THE PROMISE OF WORLD TENSIONS

THE PROMISE OF WORLD...

THE PROMISE OF

---

*To love is not to look at one another
but to look together in the same direction.*

— SAINT-EXUPÉRY

New York:

Conference on World Tensions, University of chicago, 1960.
ITT

WORLD TENSIONS

Edited by *Harlan Cleveland*

The Macmillan Company 1961

© Council on World Tensions, Inc. 1961

First Printing

The Macmillan Company, New York
Brett-Macmillan Ltd., Galt, Ontario

Printed in the United States of America

Library of Congress catalog card number: 61–8703

CONTENTS

FOREWORD

A BRASH UNDERTAKING

"How ambitious—should I say brash—is the undertaking on which we here engage: a conference on the reduction of world tensions, some being of frightening scope and intensity. An effort which might otherwise appear pretentious, is rendered indispensable by a world in desperate condition."

—RALPH J. BUNCHE

"It is a desolate thought that in the field of social and political action, of cooperation for peace on a global scale, we are not far beyond the tribal and the primitive. Man can receive a message from a gadget eight million miles away in space, which he has put there in a preordained course around the sun. But he cannot send or receive a message of peace across an Iron Curtain without someone misunderstanding or misinterpreting it. We can be so easily destroyed by this horrible imbalance in our progress."

—LESTER B. PEARSON

"Never in the history of mankind has the world been so filled with tensions as it is today, tensions between rich and poor nations, between light and dark skinned peoples, and tensions between the non-Communist and the Communist nations. We recognize that in these tensions lies a force that can, if uncontrolled, move the world toward utter disaster or, on the other

*hand, if channeled constructively, speed progress toward a better
world than we have ever had before and perhaps a better world
than we have dared dream of."*

—PAUL G. HOFFMAN

With words like these ringing in our ears, one hundred fifty
Americans and a few Canadians, Europeans, and Asians met in
May 1960 at the University of Chicago to consider the abatement
of some world tensions, and the promise of others. The driving
force behind this enterprise was Paul G. Hoffman, once leader of
the European Recovery Program and former President of the Ford
Foundation, who is now sparking into life yet another public
agency, the United Nations Special Fund. Lester B. Pearson, the
Canadian statesman who spurred the earliest efforts to make the
United Nations an operating agency as well as a debate forum,
was Conference Chairman. D. Gale Johnson, Professor of Economics at the University of Chicago, was chairman of a faculty
committee on arrangements; Margaret Grant, Executive Director of the Council on World Tensions, coordinated the preparations for the affair. Cosponsors were the University of Chicago and
World Brotherhood, Inc., which is now known as the Council on
World Tensions. The project was made possible by a grant from
The Ford Foundation to the Council.

Names make news, and in America we often measure the importance of an occasion by the density of well known figures in
attendance. By this measure the affair at Chicago was not quite
in a class with the abortive summit meeting of 1960. Yet the
names of fully one-third of the participants would have been
recognized by anyone who had followed international affairs with
interest and attention. Adlai Stevenson was there, and Carlos
Romulo, and Charles Percy who had just gone to work on the
Republican Party platform for the 1960 Presidential campaign.
And, matching a TV spectacular in its concentration of stars, six
of the eight living winners of the Nobel Peace Prize peered into
man's murky future from the same speaker's platform:

Sir Norman Angell   Nobel Peace Prize 1933
Lord John Boyd-Orr   1949
Ralph J. Bunche   1950
Lester B. Pearson   1957
Rev. Fr. Dominique Pire   1958
Philip Noel-Baker   1959

On the first day of the meetings, in a corridor choked with famous men, a young reporter for a Chicago newspaper wandered about, a bewildered look in his eye. "With so many important people here," he asked, "is anybody likely to say anything he hasn't said several times before?" It was a good question. In the deliberations that followed, I listened with that naïve and perceptive question in the back of my mind. This book contains much of what was new there, and also something of what was worth saying again.

If "names" at a conference ensure a respectful attention from the mass media, they do not guarantee that something highly significant will happen. What does make a conference useful is the quality of advance work. This Conference had been long in preparation. A seminar on "Roadblocks to Peace" was held in New York during 1957. A 1958 "working party" at Bern, Switzerland, led to two years of advance work for the 1960 meeting in Chicago. At Bern, leaders of thoughtful opinion like Henry Wriston, Philip Jessup, G. L. Mehta, Galo Plaza, Albert de Smaele, Arthur Lewis, Adlai Stevenson, Paul Hoffman, Paul Reynaud, Abol Ebtehaj, Shepard Stone and Tamon Maeda had agreed on some essential "steps toward peace" which served as a frame for the year of advance work before calling the larger meeting at Chicago. The goals of international cooperation agreed at Bern were four:

1. A *strengthened and enforceable body of world law*, requiring the abandonment or modification of reservations such as the Connally amendment and similar devices used by other nations, further technical study of the development of the law of nations by commissions in all nations and coordinated through the United Nations. A group of nations could strengthen the growth of world

law by agreeing at once, without waiting for universal acceptance, to solve their disputes according to legal principle. This goal embraces the problem of disarmament and the technical studies required before practical measures can be found for reliable and enforceable disarmament, with adequate protection for the forces of freedom and justice.

2. *Social and economic well-being of all peoples*, to be promoted through an expanding world economy, with more adequate and continuous aid to nations which need it; greater recourse to multilateral programs, including United Nations programs, for extending technical and economic aid (though recognizing that bilateral measures will still be necessary in certain circumstances); greater encouragement for local initiative by private investment; greater emphasis on helping countries to train their people for economic and social development.

3. *An open world, with freedom of travel and communication*, requiring improvement in passport and visa regulations, abolishment of censorship and other barriers to communication and free flow of ideas; studies by the United Nations or groups of international experts on the existing barriers and means of overcoming them; provision of greater resources for travel and interchange of people and ideas, through international funds with contributions from governments, foundations, business and private individuals; the strengthening of UNESCO and its work in fundamental education, technical assistance, and exchange of persons.

4. *A strengthened United Nations*, upon which more reliance must be placed in achieving all three preceding goals; the evolution of the United Nations toward eventual universal membership; further development of the United Nations fact-finding and observation bodies and bodies for maintaining peace; United Nations administration of Antarctica; and arrangements to ensure that outer space remain the domain of all nations under United Nations control.

How can these noble but rather general ideas be brought to life as national policy? For months before the 1960 meeting, experts and laymen had worked in three groups to consider ways and means. A small committee led by Ernest A. Gross, former U.S. Ambassador to the United Nations, worked on Legal Order; an Economic Development group was chaired by Paul Hoffman; and Barry Bingham, publisher of the Louisville *Courier-Journal*, headed a Communications section. In between the formal speeches at Chicago, the three sections met and hammered out policy papers for which the chairman in each case took the final responsibility. These three papers, which have been published by the Council on World Tensions, are reproduced in Chapter 9.

The background papers prepared for Chicago were individual, not committee products; for the key to useful discussion is to lay on the table propositions that have not been watered down in advance. On the whole, the lawyers were modest about what lawyers could do about world tensions; the economists were more than willing to admit how little they still know about economic development; the experts on communication admitted to some difficulty in communicating with each other. But the very modesty of the experts set a practical tone for the proceedings: if governments were to be guided by what emerged from the colloquy at Chicago, we would be closer to a condition of nonwar than we are.

The University of Chicago studies and conference were part of the continuing program of the Council on World Tensions which enlists major universities on all continents to undertake studies of the nature and causes of world tensions from regional and international viewpoints. The studies serve as a basis for discussion by outstanding educators, public leaders, businessmen and professional men and women. From these discussions come specific recommendations for action toward peace which the Council disseminates widely on all levels—ranging from school teachers to heads of governments. During 1961, the Council will cooperate with the University of Bombay and Oxford University in Asian and European counterparts to the North American Chicago project.

Except for Chapter 1, the material in this book was produced for the Council on World Tensions, whose permission to use it is gratefully acknowledged. The headquarters of the Council on World Tensions are located at 304 East 42nd Street in New York City.

Chapter 1 was written after the Conference. A part of it was published as a guest-editorial in the *Saturday Review* (July 16, 1960), and is included here by permission. It is in no sense a summary of Conference thinking, but rather the reflections of one individual who was there. Some of the participants might not have had the same reaction; but to one observer, the striking thing about the Conference was the consensus that all the world's tensions are not bad, fit only to be reduced.

H. C.

Syracuse, New York
August 20, 1960

NOTES ON THE CONTRIBUTORS

Pulitzer Prize Winner HARRY ASHMORE resigned in 1959 from the executive editorship of the Little Rock, Arkansas, *Gazette* to become a consultant to the Center for the Study of Democratic Institutions at Santa Barbara, California. This project has recently been established by the Fund for the Republic to study basic issues in American society, including the mass communications media and their role. Mr. Ashmore's book, *An Epitaph for Dixie*, received major recognition for foresighted commentary on racial and related problems in the Southern United States.

Editor-in-Chief BARRY BINGHAM of the Louisville *Courier-Journal* and the Louisville *Times* has spent his professional newspaper career, which began when he became a police reporter, in his native city. He has served as chief of the Economic Cooperation Administration's mission to France and as ECA deputy administrator at large to all participating countries. On the national scene, Mr. Bingham headed national volunteers for Stevenson groups both in 1952 and 1956 and accompanied Mr. Stevenson on his 1953 world tour. Among his many distinguished positions is his membership on the Pulitzer Prize Advisory Board.

Under-Secretary RALPH BUNCHE is likely to be among the first representatives of the United Nations in a troubled area. His work in the Near East earned him the Nobel Peace Prize and in 1960 he made multiple trips into the Congo attempting to alleviate tensions there. Dr. Bunche's M.A. and Ph.D. are from Harvard. He rose to be chief of the African section of the Office of Strategic Services during World War II, moved over to the State Department in 1944 and in 1946 became director of the United Nations Trusteeship Division. His knowledge includes expertise in such areas as colonial policy, trusteeships, and race relations.

Dean HARLAN CLEVELAND of the Maxwell Graduate School of Citizenship and Public Affairs, Syracuse University, concerns himself with a wide range of public activities. He writes, speaks, and teaches about administration, economic development, and U.S. foreign policy. He is coauthor of *The Art of Overseasmanship* and *The Overseas Americans*. A graduate of Princeton and a Rhodes Scholar at Oxford University, Dean Cleveland spent eleven years as a U.S. Government official, mostly in foreign operations, and two more as an overseas administrator for the United Nations Relief and Rehabilitation Administration. Between his government and academic careers he was executive editor, then publisher, of *The Reporter* magazine. He has been Dean of the Maxwell School since 1956.

Attorney ERNEST GROSS includes among his clients United Nations Secretary-General Dag Hammerskjold for whom he acts as legal advisor. Mr. Gross, former United States Ambassador to the United Nations and previously Assistant Secretary of State, has had an international legal education, first at Harvard, then at Oxford, and finally at the Geneva School of International Studies. He has served as counsel to the National Association of Manufacturers and the National Labor Relations Board. He is also a trustee of the Carnegie Endowment for International Peace and a director of the Council on World Tensions.

Professor LOUIS HENKIN is a former law clerk to both Learned Hand and Felix Frankfurter. He was admitted to Supreme

Court practice in 1947 and in that same year became a consultant to the United Nations Legal Department. Among his offerings at the University of Pennsylvania Law School, where he has taught since 1958, are seminars in international transactions, the law of American foreign affairs, and recent constitutional developments. He is the author of *Arms Control and Inspection*.

Managing Director PAUL G. HOFFMAN of the United Nations' Special Fund has had a multiple career as salesman, industrialist, high government official, foundation head, and political advisor. A native of Chicago, his business career started as a filling station operator and brought him to the chairmanship of the Studebaker Corporation. As first administrator of the Economic Cooperation Administration, much of the credit for making the Marshall Plan a reality was his. Later he served for a time as president of the Ford Foundation and as chairman of the Fund for the Republic. Mr. Hoffman's United Nations activities have included service as a delegate to the General Assembly as well as his present post with the Special Fund. He is a director of the Council on World Tensions. Mr. Hoffman has also found time to be the author of two books, *Seven Roads to Safety* (1937) and *Peace Can Be Won* (1951) and numerous articles and pamphlets.

Principal W. ARTHUR LEWIS, born on the island of St. Lucia, British West Indies, now heads the University College of the West Indies at Jamaica. His tricontinental bihemispheric career includes teaching at the London School of Economics and the University of Manchester, being Economic Advisor to the Prime Minister of Ghana, and holding various positions with the British government at London and the United Nations in the Far East, the Gold Coast, and Nigeria. Until March, 1960, he was Deputy Managing Director of the United Nations' Special Fund. His books include *Principles of Economic Planning* (1959) and *The Theory of Economic Grants* (1955).

LESTER B. PEARSON, now leader of Canada's Liberal party, was born in Toronto and graduated from the University of Toronto and Oxford University. During his diplomatic and political career, Mr. Pearson has served as Canadian Ambassador to the United States, Secretary of State for External Affairs, and President of the United Nations General Assembly from 1952 to 1953. He was awarded the 1957 Nobel Peace Prize for his leadership in the United Nations effort to end the British-French-Israeli invasion of Suez. Mr. Pearson was Chancellor of Victoria University in Toronto from 1951 to 1958 and has received honorary degrees from many universities, including Toronto, Yale, Princeton, Ceylon, Columbia, and Harvard. He is the author of two books, *Democracy in World Politics* (1955) and *Diplomacy in the Nuclear Age* (1959). Having served as Chairman of the Conference on World Tensions, Mr. Pearson is now International Executive Chairman of the Council on World Tensions.

Professor EUGENE RABINOWITCH is known both as a scientist and a writer. His advanced degree was conferred by the University of Berlin—he was born in St. Petersburg, Russia—and he has taught at the University of Göttingen and London, and the Massachusetts Institute of Technology; since 1947, he has been at the University of Illinois. The author of many scholarly books and journal articles, his *Minutes to Midnight* reflected the fears and expectations of a scientist who had been part of the Manhattan Project and who had seen the accumulations of vast power in the hands of men not acclimated to its use. He is editor of the *Bulletin of the Atomic Scientists*.

Former Governor ADLAI STEVENSON's eloquence on a wide range of public affairs is only slightly less familiar to non-Americans than it is to Americans. His two campaigns for the Presidency, his visits overseas, and his many writings and public appearances, have placed him at the articulate forefront of reason in the midst of unreasonableness. His ability to illuminate human entanglements is no more clearly seen than in his chapter, "Full Promise of a Distracted World." Before gaining national prominence during a highly successful term as Governor of Illinois, Stevenson was a journalist, lawyer, and advisor to various government agencies, including the State Department. He served as a member of the U.S. delegation in the establishment of the United Nations.

Professor IRVING SWERDLOW holds an award from the Burmese government for his work there in drawing up a program for economic development. He has also, in addition to other government positions, been a member of the United States delegation to both the North Atlantic Treaty Organization and the Office of European Economic Cooperation. Educated at the University of North Dakota, New York University, American University, and the University of Wisconsin, he now teaches at the Maxwell Graduate School, Syracuse University, where he is closely associated with Dean Harlan Cleveland in the direction of a study of cross-cultural operations being conducted under a Ford Foundation grant.

I

THE DIALOGUE OF THE DEAF

Harlan Cleveland

What quality of vision, what hints about how to organize world society, emerge when six certified men of peace share a platform, to speak of their past and of our future? It happened at Chicago, at the Conference on World Tensions, and it was a curious experience: dispiriting if one came looking for new answers, confusing if one looked for a common denominator among the six. Yet if the listener put aside his passion for program and procedure, and attended merely to the spirit of the enterprise, the coming together of six-eighths of the living winners of the Nobel Peace Prize was full of meaning and not merely spectacular.

Nearing eighty, Albert Schweitzer felt unable to make the tiring passage to Chicago. Ninety-three-year-old Emily Balch, international women's leader, was absent too. But with or without them, it was almost embarrassingly obvious that the Nobel committee generally finds peaceful men in the Atlantic Community and the Christian quarter of the world. A Canadian, a Scotsman, two Englishmen, a Belgian, and an American shared the platform: two politicians, two international administrators, a publicist, and a priest.

The shadow of atomic uncertainty hung heavy over the long evening; each speaker echoed Karl Jaspers' gloomy words of a

1

generation ago: "A dread of life perhaps unparalleled in its intensity is modern man's sinister companion," he wrote—and the scientists had not even split the atom then. Yet the Nobel Prize winners spoke with the eloquence of busy lives and the conviction that the jig is not up. These men do not despair for man's future; despair is a self-indulgence from which the Nobel Peace laureates seem to achieve a lifelong immunity. Man, they seemed to say, has tiptoed his way through so many dangers: "Glittering generality that it is," said Ralph Bunche, "I do have faith that at least the good sense if not always the good in man will prevail."

Dread brings on a preoccupation with what is dreaded, so it was not surprising to find most of the laureates talking about disarmament. They agreed with President Eisenhower's simple but eloquent summary of the modern dilemma: "There is no alternative to peace."

"Surely," said Lester Pearson, "we have no choice but to rule out war itself as a tolerable situation for any international problem. Surely we must accept the inescapable fact—and base our policies on it—that there is now no alternative to the peaceful and negotiated solution of every international problem. Acceptance in theory is one thing—and not difficult. Conversion of that acceptance into policy is something else. Yet if great and powerful nations reject this policy and instead insist on the right to use force at their own command, they can destroy their enemies, themselves, and everybody else. Who then is the realist, who the visionary?"

"If the tensions of the past persist into the nuclear age they will destroy us," added Sir Norman Angell. "World authority there must be, if we are to survive."

The objective is clear, if one stands at a great distance from it: something called peace, viewed by too many people as an object to be pursued, not an operation to be conducted. "World authority there must be," Sir Norman affirmed; Lord Boyd-Orr wanted "equal and rapid disarmament." But how? The procedural suggestions were lacking that evening, even from men who in their time have invented imaginative procedures for dealing with international tensions in the real world.

The closest thing to a description of procedures for peace was Philip Noel-Baker's nostalgic assessment of the League of Nations —a story he discreetly refrained from carrying beyond 1932. The League stopped four wars after large-scale fighting had begun, and settled scores of other disputes through political mediation or the work of the World Court. But the 1932 Disarmament Conference collapsed—and it was all downhill after that. The United Nations is now at the 1932 stage; as Frank Graham recently summed it up:

> With all its inadequacies and frustrations, the United Nations has so far helped to prevent the beginning of a third world war, has cooled off six hot spots on the earth where a local fire might have become a global conflagration, and carries on with small budgets great campaigns of enlightenment and technical aid against poverty, hunger, illiteracy, disease, unfair discrimination, colonialism, armaments, and the war system itself.

The importance of the United Nations has been frequently reasserted by men like Carlos Romulo, who also attended the conference. His persistent espousal of the United Nations as "a great cause and a great opportunity" can scarcely be recalled too often. "Let the United Nations be given the opportunity to do its share," he asked, knowing that if this could be done some tensions would be diverted to a channel designed to handle them. Yet the arms race still plagues the UN, as it did the League. The Nobel Peace laureates know they are for disarmament, because in the Atlantic Community that is simply part of being for peace. It is the next step which eludes them, as it does the rest of us.

The evening's most eloquent speech was made in French by the Belgian priest, Father Dominique Pire. He spoke of the responsibility he felt as winner of the Nobel Prize, citing in support a Nobel Prize winner in literature, Albert Camus: "The world in which I live fills me with aversion, but I find myself bound on all sides by Men who suffer there." Father Pire went on to complain that the Asians, the Africans, and the Communists were absent from the audience, and vowed not to support "any motion which the conscience of the absentees would not accept"—a posture of guaranteed inaction on any relevant subject which contradicted his own fine affirmation fifteen minutes earlier: "I dare to believe that men could get along well by mutually admitting their contradictions." Father Pire then suggested that "the cause of peace" would be advanced by a meeting between the Nobel laureates and the winners of the Stalin Peace Prize. Again he seemed to contradict himself: earlier he had warned against the sentimentality of "the open heart and the closed eye."

Sentiment, nostalgia, and generalized exhortations were not a convincing substitute for policy that night. The Nobel laureates produced no magic answers. Yet something of great importance was symbolized by those six men sitting in a row in the bleak light of a university auditorium. Most of them were honored, after all, not for the eloquence of their words but for the practical things they had done—in the improvement of nutrition, in Middle East diplomacy, in domestic and international politics, in building "European villages" out of broken men. Sir Norman Angell, whose contribution to international peace has been a powerful torrent of words about it, found the words to stress the greater importance of action, of "next steps" which can cumulatively change the nature of man himself:

The emotions which are part of the explanation of our political errors are very ancient, very deeply rooted in human nature. Yet experience proves they can be profoundly changed by culture, a culture in which our schools have played little part, and higher learning even less. How small the part of learning, erudition, a glance at history reveals. Greece could produce an immortal political literature we still study. But it could not maintain peace between its own city states. In the modern world the most intensely schooled nation of all chose

Hitler for its master. The churches of Christendom could proclaim the message of the Prince of Peace, a message of mercy, pity, compassion, brotherhood. Learned theologians elaborated it in a mountainous theological literature, added to century after century. But the learned theologians fought each other, using the weapons of torture and death, the rack, burning alive, the prolonged religious war. Earlier centuries showed other aspects of the human spirit. For thousands of years men believed that God, or the Gods, would be pleased if children were cut to pieces with stone knives on Holy Altars.

All that has gone, at least in the West. Human sacrifice is no more; religious wars have ceased; the torture chambers are closed. It is an immense change. What was once right has become wrong, what was wrong, right. Religion has not been destroyed and religious differences remain. But the ordinary unlearned man knows that true religion cannot be promoted by one army defeating another; he knows that the real defense of religious truth is not military but psychological. How has a change so profound taken place in the minds of the multitude?

The question is vital because the means which have brought peace between rival religious groups are the only means now left to us in the nuclear age for bringing about peace between rival political groups, between one kind of society and another.

2

At first the subject for Chicago was "the reduction of world tensions." But some objected: are not some tensions, on balance, a Good Thing? Granting that war tensions leading to nuclear destruction must be reduced for simple survival, what are we to say of the passion for equality, the revolution of rising economic hopes, the aspirations for those strange but precious goals, Free-Dom and In-De-Pen-Dence? "If channeled constructively" these are the promising tensions, the ambition and incentive that drive men to take their worldly destiny in their own hands.

The promising tensions are first of all personal, the product of the individual's perception of a frustrating gap between the reality of his situation and his vision of what might be. The basic wants of modern man might be categorized as follows:

First, modern man wants a sense of welfare and security—a minimum standard of "enough" in material living. How much is "enough" will vary from society to society and from decade to decade. But at any moment in any society there will exist (even if it cannot be precise) a practical definition of the minimum standard which the society will collectively seek for its every individual member.

Second, modern man wants a sense of equity and justice—the feeling that he is being treated justly, not as measured by some ultimate standard but as measured against the treatment accorded to other people regarded as in comparable conditions.

Third, modern man wants a sense of achievement and opportunity—man's feeling that he is getting somewhere, that the group of which he is a part is making progress toward goals in which he feels some emotional involvement.

Fourth, modern man wants a sense of participation and purpose—the feeling that he has some control over his own destiny through taking part in a group or groups that can and do in fact influence the basic decisions on which his welfare, equity, and achievement depend—decisions about the state of the economy, the security of person, the freedom of mind, and ultimately about life and death, peace and war.

The basic wants of man are not statistically determinable or empirically verifiable in general. They are all "feelings," or "senses," based on vague judgments about the relationship of the individual and his needs to the society in which he finds himself. Even for a small group at a defined time in a particular place, the judgments about adequacy, equity, achievement and participation must be rough approximations, not "facts" which can be proven.

The aspirations of modern man are the product of an awareness by the individual of his relationship to society. They imply that he cares about this relationship, that his attitude is of one seeking to influence his destiny, not passively accepting what Fate or the gods or his own family have provided in the way of environment. It hardly needs to be observed that the intensity of this awareness is a new state of mind for most of mankind, dating for most societies from the Renaissance and the Reformation in the West, spreading to the East through colonial governors, district officers, navies and armies, missionaries and traders.

The basic wants are appropriate to an era in which, as Charles Frankel puts it, we don't know where we are going, but we know we are going there fast. We know that an ever higher standard of welfare is technically possible, that greater equity can be achieved in a situation of growth. The very urge for a sense of achievement is evidence that change is the expected norm. The growing desire to participate in decisions affecting our own destiny stems from the conviction that things are certain to change and that events must therefore be influenced in directions that are congenial to us.

But the fact that man's aspirations are geared to rapid change does not mean that they are necessarily geared to each other. It is one thing to compare reality with a vision, and quite another to organize a society to take advantage of the opportunities its members can clearly perceive.

Breaking through the gloomy images of atomic annihilation, the recurring theme at the 1960 Conference on World Tensions was a sense of new tasks to be tackled, tasks that might prove so relevant to man's hopes that they would bypass man's fears— bypass the spyings and the summits, the arms race and even the disarmament talks. It was this emerging spirit of qualified optimism —qualified by the determination to create a sounder basis for optimism, that made something worth-while and important of the brash undertaking at Chicago.

"We are experimenting," said Albert de Smaele of Belgium; "let us recognize it in all humility. And let us recognize that we are all bound by the success or failure of this gigantic *essai*. Is it not imperative that in such vital and dramatic instance we should thoroughly exchange our observation sheets?"

3

Before we can make sense of our actions for peace, we need to get into perspective our talking about peace. Talking with the Russians is by no means the most important work we have to do in the world. But before we pass to more vital matters, let us consider summitry, this curious new form of diplomacy, the open disagreement openly arrived at. Father Dominique Pire used a phrase that well described it: *le dialogue des sourds,* the dialogue of the deaf.

The mutual deafness is a double infirmity, on both sides. It is not just that the Russians cannot hear us and we cannot hear them—though our mutual soundproofing is by itself a serious enough threat to the world's destiny. But the deafness is domestic as well as international. Within the Soviet Union, a solicitous government, anxious not to have its citizens disturbed by hearing different views of man and society, stops their ears as a matter of policy. In the United States, on the other hand, freedom is untrammeled—freedom of the government to put its foot in its mouth, the freedom of the citizen to listen to so many other things, from advertising jingles at 7:00 A.M. to Jack Paar at midnight, that he cannot hear the ticking of destiny's time clock.

Given all the competing noise, we naturally pay attention to international diplomacy only when it fairly screams for us to listen. And that means we mostly listen to the wrong subjects at the wrong times.

Consider the Great Fiasco of 1960, the abortive summit meeting in Paris. An ill-prepared and ill-fated conference was widely represented as fateful and historic. We were led (by our government and our newspapers and our own hopes) to believe that because several very important people were assembled there, the summit meeting was the most important happening in the international world.

That was precisely what the Soviet strategists wanted us to believe, for the Soviets have discovered our Achilles' heel: a fatal weakness for paying attention to only one crisis at a time. The Russians learned, almost by accident, that if they build one big irrelevant bonfire to attract our fascinated gaze, we will forget to do most of the other things we should be doing. Or, to change the image, the Soviets have learned what every motorist knows: that if the opposing car turns its headlights up bright, there is an almost irresistible temptation to look at the oncoming headlights, rather than at the road to be traveled. The bright, glaring beacon from Berlin served to take our eyes off Asia, Africa, and Latin America for close to two years—and Cuba and the Congo have provided other sharp reminders of what prolonged neglect can accomplish.

For a dozen years now, we have repeatedly fallen into the same bear-trap. Starting in 1946 with Russian threats to Turkey and the attempt to take over Iran's northern province of Azerbaijan, there has been a continuous series of trumped-up crises, but always one at a time: the Berlin blockade, the invasion of South Korea, the Indochina war, the attack on Quemoy and the Matsu Islands, the threat to Laos, the Berlin threat again. It is arguable that the whole Korean War was justified, from the point of view of the leaders of world communism, solely by its success in causing the United States to lose its enthusiasm for the dangerously popular, too constructive line of policy represented by the Marshall Plan in Europe and the beginnings of aid to Asia, Africa, and Latin America under the Point Four program. Starting the day after the Korean War broke out, we tried to wrap our whole foreign policy around something called "mutual security," which made military preparations the centerpiece of American foreign policy. Our preoccupation with hot and cold running wars, in turn, enormously complicated the task of relating ourselves to the uncommitted nations whose main interest, naturally, was in their own development and not in our public wrestling match with the Russians.

Summit meetings are, to be sure, somewhat less dangerous than military aggression as a way of building large irrelevant bonfires to mesmerize us. What *is* serious is our tendency to take so seriously a gambit that is largely calculated to take our minds off our work. Note the technique carefully. The Soviets have been beating the drum for a meeting at the summit on Berlin, during the very period when their own position on Berlin has been hardening, not softening. The Berlin issue had already been stalemated for fifteen years. Neither the Western powers nor the Kremlin have ever shown, during this whole period, the slightest intention of giving up their respective positions there. None of the so-called preparations for the summit meeting made the slightest dent in the essential position of either side.

What was true of Berlin was true of the broader issue of German unification: neither side was willing to recede from long-established positions. Nevertheless, the unification of Germany has been a staple subject of diplomatic conversation ever since the end of World War II. It surely has not been worth more than a fraction of the time and energy we have devoted to discussing it —not because unification is unimportant but because it obviously is not going to happen while the Russians are sitting on the heads of the East Germans. Yet every Secretary of State since James Byrnes has acted as if it were the main subject on the broad international agenda. And as a consequence, these Secretaries of State have not found the time and energy and interest to address themselves often enough and vigorously enough to troubles in the Far East, to mobilizing support for the Indian Five-Year Plans, to constructive steps toward peace in the Middle East, to the building of effective new governments in the emerging nations of Africa, to the nurturing of economic growth and political democracy in Latin America.

In short, we have spent much of the past decade talking with the Communists about subjects of their choosing, rather than acting on the subjects of our own choosing. The world's power structure is not going to be changed by what we say to the Communists; it is going to be changed by what we do in those parts of the world we *can* reach by promoting rapid economic development, by the calm intent to resist aggression anywhere, by the repeated demonstration that neither diplomatic truculence nor military power will get Communists anywhere, by their gradual realization that world domination is simply not within their grasp, and never will be.

This is not to say that we should not talk with the Communists anywhere and everywhere, at every possible level, about any matter that seems to be in the slightest degree negotiable. Our willingness to talk at unreasonable length with anybody is an essential part of our posture of peace. But we should not, for this purpose, engage the full attention of our first team. The President should not get involved in conversations that have not been so thoroughly prepared ahead of time that some measure of real accommodation among the summiteers is assured. At the Foreign Ministers level, we must somehow preserve the Secretary of State (and his opposite members in Canada and Western Europe) from permanent incarceration in meeting rooms.

To avoid sentencing him to this fate, perhaps a new position should be created in the U.S. Government, a Cabinet post of Joint Secretary of State. The man filling this post must be willing and able to spend his entire time, assisted by a full-time professional staff, talking with the Soviets and the Chinese and anybody else he can persuade to listen to him about disarmament, Berlin, and other subjects on which mutual loquacity for the time being exceeds mutual understanding.

These arrangements would free the President and the Secretary of State, and their regular staffs, for the massive and exciting task of helping to create, on the free side of the talking curtain, contagiously successful societies that will give the lie to the Communist claims of invincibility and inevitability.

4

If we can free ourselves from the hypnotic effect of summitry, and get used to the idea that our main job in foreign affairs is to help other nations build successful free societies, then the decade ahead of us holds exciting prospects indeed.

It is still a fact, in spite of all our industrial progress and all our humanistic words, that for most human beings the world is a miserable place. It is a fact that communism, which has not caused this problem, seeks to use it as a weapon against the ways of freedom. Within the countries of the West, the administrators of democracy have disproved Marx's famous prediction that the rich would get richer and the poor would get poorer. But in the world at large, we have yet to disprove Lenin's brilliant adaptation of the Marxian dogma—the prediction that the rich *nations* would get richer and the poor *nations* poorer. In some of the poor nations things have quite literally grown worse, not better, in recent years. And more and more people have become aware of their misery by the very contrast of their own lot with our unprecedented and still growing prosperity.

Yet we have not resolved to guarantee the economic growth of the free world, though we quite literally have the power to do so in concert with our Western democratic friends. We are not doing it yet on a serious scale because we have not yet decided *why* we should do it. And in democratic politics, it is not enough to decide to act, we have to decide why we are prepared to act.

So far, we have been giving ourselves only one main reason for exercising the leadership which has fallen to us. That one reason is the challenge of Russian competition. Our leaders have been acting as though fear of the Russians is the only dependable motivation that will assure wide public support of any major foreign policy move. But dread is always too narrow a base for public support of what the government needs to do. Even in wartime, when the basis for fear is obvious, the American people have had to be moved by positive appeals to hope for a better future: Wilson summoned us to make the world safe for democracy, Franklin Roosevelt bade us guarantee the Four Freedoms to all men.

In our time and place, the most dramatic appeal to fear seems to move Americans the least. The Civil Defense people rest their case for public concern on scaring us to life, but their efforts are merely boring to most people, though they produce neurotic reactions in a few. Like the Ghost of Hamlet's father, the Civil Defense people proclaim that the truth about the danger we face is too highly classified to discuss, but they can assure us it is incredibly frightening:

> But that I am forbid
> To tell the secrets of my prison-house,
> I could a tale unfold whose lightest word
> Would harrow up thy soul, freeze thy young blood,
> Make thy two eyes, like stars, start from their spheres,
> Thy knotted and combined locks to part
> And each particular hair to stand on end
> Like quills upon the fretful porpentine:
> But this eternal blazon must not be
> To ears of flesh and blood. List, list, O list!

Hamlet certainly listened, but the vague and fearsome things the Ghost told him did not galvanize him into constructive and useful action; they made him nervous, unpredictable, and in the end, self-destroying. Fear-driven anticommunism does, of course, provide a short-run spur to action, but it also produces neurotic actions and, in the long run, bad policy.

Fortunately, we are quite capable of doing things for more than one reason at the same time. If the United States foreign-aid programs still, in spite of everything, retain some genuine public appeal, it is because they are not only part of the Mutual Security Program but also part of the American tradition of humanitarian action, with an impressive degree of political support from church groups, labor unions, women's organizations, and other groups that think of themselves as the conscience of the nation. American foreign operations are both good anticommunism and good humanitarianism—and for the farmers and some businessmen, they are good business, too. It is in the nature of our pluralistic society that we normally have plural reasons, even mutually conflicting reasons, for taking any major action in our public and international affairs.

Beyond all the obvious reasons for acting more vigorously to make sure the poor countries get richer, there is one that our leaders do not usually make speeches about, because it is so hard to express without sounding sentimental. The truth is that *we* need this kind of action, even more than our friends in the less developed areas need to have us take it. We need it for our own morale. We need it because it is the next big national effort (short of war) into which we can throw our immense and restless American energies. It is the successor to the Revolutionary War, the opening of the West, the struggle over the Union, the freeing of the slaves, the molding of industrial power, the acquisition of the Philippines and the Open Door in China, the trust-busting frenzy and the conservation crusade, the New Freedom and the New Deal, the war to save democracy and the war to establish the United Nations, the Marshall Plan for European recovery and Point Four, that first glimmering of concern for the non-European world.

We have to get on with the job of proving that people can get welfare, security, justice, and a sense of achievement through participation in free institutions managed by leaders they can choose —and replace. We have to do this to validate our own profound convictions about the nature of man and his proper relationship to society. For the words which express our deepest aspirations—

words like liberty, equality, brotherhood, the dignity of man— must be constantly repurchased on the open market of public action. Words like these have always had to be bought and re- bought, as Stephen Vincent Benét once reminded us,

> . . . with belief and passion, at great cost.
> They were bought with the bitter and anonymous blood
> Of farmers, teachers, shoemakers and fools
> Who broke the old rule and the pride of kings.
> It took a long time to buy these words.
> It took a long time to buy them and much pain.

Some of the world's tensions may indeed be too taut for comfort. But for Americans, the first task of all is not to reduce other people's tensions. It is rather to increase our own: to tighten our resolve and heighten our sense of urgency about the promise (not merely the danger) of the only world we live in.

The problem of the Arms Race, fiercer and more costly now than ever before, still gathers pace and momentum every year: The Arms Race, a deep-seated and very potent cause of all the tensions which we know today.

Abolition of the immense machinery of devastating and instantaneous surprise attack would mean a major revolution in the conduct of international affairs. But who doubts that a major revolution is required? Who doubts that modern arms have destroyed all hope of national defense?

If history repeats itself today, we can be very certain that the instruments of democratic government, of government of the people, by the people, for the people, will tragically, and it may be finally, have failed.

—PHILIP NOEL-BAKER

TOWARD A "RULE OF LAW" COMMUNITY

Louis Henkin

Ours is hardly a world at peace. If the principal "war" is a "cold war," yet there is not peace. In the tensions between East and West, aggravated by awesome destructive power on both sides, in equally sharp if less pervasive tensions among smaller nations, lie serious dangers and threats to peace. There are tensions also, and seeds of tension, in the growth of new nationalisms, in the drive of previously non-self-governing people for independence, in the demand of these peoples and other peoples for a greater share of the world's goods and a better life.

To these special sources of tension are added those ever-present in a society of sovereign states with competing economic and political interests. These tensions may lead to the use or threat of force, as recently in Suez. If not force, there may be other retaliation. In any event, there is "injustice." In all events, tension results. The threat of war is pervasive. The sense of order, of justice under law, is largely lacking. There is dis-ease among nations, which, even if it should not in fact erupt into war, poisons relations in the world family.

To cure this disease, men of good will turn to "the law," seeking in its concepts, institutions, methods, and mechanics, ways to reduce the threat of war and to enhance international order. And lawyers have responded to this challenge, although different lawyers have responded in different ways. Some have concentrated on ultimate goods, on optimum solutions and programs. They speak almost yearningly of the "rule of law." They respond to a common wish that there shall be a world community with the hallmarks and trappings of law that are known domestically in enlightened Western countries—a community observing accepted rules of conduct between nations; courts applying these rules in cases or controversies not settled amicably by the parties; police to enforce, if necessary, the law as decided by the courts. And so lawyers have formulated, and continue to refine, principles of conduct for nations in a community of nations. They have proposed and developed processes for giving effect to such principles, and programs for applying and administering these processes, and for enforcing the rules of conduct against recalcitrant nations. They concentrate on the development of new rules where none exist, or where present rules are deemed unsatisfactory. They develop and strengthen statutes for international adjudicatory tribunals. They propose new and renewed charters for international organization and police.

Those who devote their efforts to these goals recognize that wishing for or proclaiming a rule of law does not create in fact a law of nations. They are aware that, in a society of sovereign states, an established order of laws and courts and police—which does not effectively exist even within many domestic societies—is at best a dream to be approximated, and there appears little immediate prospect that nations will agree to give up much of their present sovereignty. But those who labor in this vineyard believe that it is important to keep ultimate goals in sight; that plans and blueprints make it more likely that such a world can be achieved, at least that more progress can be made toward it; that significant educational and even political benefits may derive from reminding nations and peoples how the world might look.

Other lawyers, concerned for the growth and enhancing of international order through law, begin from different positions, give different emphases. They stress that law does not create a World Community; it can only reflect such a community if it exists. In today's world, sharply polarized between East and West, there is not even the foundation for a common society to support a common law. The rule of law, in an ultimate sense, is an ideal state of health, not a prescription for achieving it. The question indeed is how, in a sorely divided world, one can achieve even a small measure of this health. If substantial order is to come without another world holocaust, it must grow from present roots. If it is to be planned, it can only be built on and projected out of the present foundations. Will East and West, with divergent and perhaps inconsistent interests, accept common standards of action, common methods and machinery for enforcing or vindicating these standards? Rules exist, but are they rules which the leading nations, and the new nations, recognize and observe? There are institutions and procedures—judicial, quasi-judicial, or political, multilateral or bilateral—but will nations use them and abide by their outcome?

The East and the West do not agree on many rules; they do not accept courts or other impartial forums to decide disputes; there is no power to compel either side to abide by any rules or decisions, and frequently no voluntary acceptance of them. Although the West has been far more amenable to rules, and more reluctant to incur the onus in world opinion of breaching them, it too may act in disregard of "law" where it feels important interests are at stake. Even the smaller nations find it easier to disregard law as a result of the lack of a strong fabric of a society of nations, or because of the lack of agreed force on behalf of the "law" and the world community, or because there is a big champion who might defend their violations. The nations newly come to independence may have serious question as to the meaning for them of old concepts and institutions; will they agree to accept them? Will they seek changes to which other nations could agree?

If there is no perfect order and law in today's society of nations, some law, some standards of behavior observed, some machinery for vindicating these standards, do in fact exist. This "law" has strengths and has enjoyed successes. It has serious weaknesses and has suffered defeats. It needs strengthening. It can be strengthened in ways that reflect the world of today, that take account of power and other facts of international life, that reflect the different interests of different nations, as they see their interests.

Law can be achieved to the extent that it is in the common interest of nations, if nations can be made to recognize that it is in their common interests. In a world dominated by two powerful giants, law can be achieved if, and to the extent that, these powers believe that it is in their interests to achieve it. What is required, then, is to persuade nations, particularly the Big Powers, that order and law, at least in some areas, are in their interest. There must be an identification of areas of such coincidence of interest—common interest in having standards of conduct, explicit or tacit, upon given subjects, common interests in the substance of the standards, common interests, especially, in procedures for implementing or applying these standards, as well as procedures for settling disputes in areas where there are no agreed rules.

There are in fact significant areas of coincidence of interest between East and West within which some "law" exists, and more can be developed. There are wider areas of coincidence of interest between old nations and new, and therefore hope and need for development of legal and political institutions and practices in relations between them. And, finally, there are still larger areas of even deeper coincidence of interest among the Western nations with common values and traditions where law exists and can grow importantly, which would also serve as an example and a focus for extending the rule of law to other countries, other areas and groups. The concepts, methods, and tools of law, we believe, can be invoked to increase the areas of international activity which are subject to law, and therefore contribute to the lessening or arresting of existing tensions, to the prevention of new tensions. The lawyer in close concert with economists and leaders in other disciplines concerned with the cooperation of people and communications among them, can contribute not only in his capacity as outstanding citizen and leader, but through the lawyer's skills and insights—in negotiation and adjustment, in the development and formulation of standards of conduct, in devising procedures for giving effect to such standards, in applying and administering these procedures.

2

The tendency to think of the Rule of Law as denoting a complete system of rules and courts and police has diverted attention from the amount and kind of law that in fact exists. Without stopping to debate what is a proper definition of law, it should be clear that there is a substantial order, and that it gives some promise of continuing.

Rules have existed between nations, perhaps since before the recorded history of nations and of compacts between them. The law of nations of older times, and modern international law, and comity and custom, reflect some rules which have acceptability to this day. There are thousands of treaties, bilateral and multilateral, establishing agreed standards which are very largely observed. Some nations have set themselves standards and live by them. Procedures and machinery too have developed. If international courts are new and still of limited effectiveness, courts are hardly the only or ultimately the best vehicle for maintaining or vindicating order. The exchange of ambassadors and embassies and communications represents an ancient and effective form and forum for negotiation for settlement of disputes in the light of underlying rules or standards of conduct. Mediation or conciliation by others, and arbitration before some acceptable third party, are old forms of giving effect to law. The recent establishment of other tribunals, of political bodies—notably the United Nations—to deal with political disputes, is an important indication and manifestation of law and order. And there is the International Court of Justice, weak though it may be.

Even the most critical area of international relations—the avoidance of war and of the use of force—is not devoid of law. Insofar as there is coincidence of interest, there is some law and order. But such law needs strengthening in important respects.

The Charter of the United Nations outlaws aggressive war. It forbids nations, in effect, to initiate the use of force. All members bind themselves "to refrain in their international relations from the threat or use of force against the territorial integrity or political independence of any state, or in any other manner inconsistent with the purposes of the United Nations." (Article 2, section 4.) They bind themselves "to settle their international disputes by peaceful means in such a manner that international peace and security, and justice, are not endangered." (Article 2, section 3.) Except when it is acting at the behest of the United Nations in support of the purposes of the Charter, a nation may use force only in the exercise of "the inherent right of individual or collective self-defense if an armed attack occurs against a Member of the United Nations. . . ." (Article 51.)

Here are rules of law. These are not vague principles of an old "international law" developed in the West of centuries ago. They are not principles of capitalism or of colonial power. They are new principles adopted after World War II by all nations, East and West, Communist and non-Communist, old and new. The nations just born and those about to be born promptly and eagerly seek membership in the UN, and pledge adherence to the UN Charter and its fundamental purpose of outlawing the use of force in relations between nations.

There is, we believe, a coincidence of interest—between East and West, and with all nations—on this rule against the use of force. Surely there is common interest in avoiding total war and total devastation. And any substantial use of force between nations

today can only too readily lead to total war. In the present
international context there is a common interest also in
being and appearing to be law-observant in this fundamental
respect. While there may be some skepticism whether all
nations are indeed "true believers," whether they truly desire to observe these rules of "no force," it is yet significant that
nations unanimously and for the first time feel obliged to proclaim
and preach this "gospel" and maintain their adherence to it. In
fact, there has been greater observance of the rule than is sometimes recognized; the exceptions—Palestine, Korea, Suez, Hungary
—can be explained, although not, of course, justified. (In Korea
and Suez—and in the Palestine area generally—peace was restored,
some order established, law largely vindicated.) If it be said that it
is fear, not piety, that supports this rule of law, that it is NATO
not the UN which is its principal shield, that it is the threat of
mutual or self-destruction which alone has saved the world from
war, yet it is a fact that to date we have been largely saved. There
is observance of the rule; there is some basis for confidence that it
will continue to be observed. This too is law. For whatever reasons,
by recognized means, machinery, procedures, the law of the UN
Charter generally prevails.

This is not to suggest that there is cause for complacence that
terrible war will not come. If world tension today is, in a sense, a
happy reflection of the fact that the conflicting interests which
have created tensions have not erupted into war, yet the existence
of these tensions is a continuing reminder of the threat of war,
deliberate or accidental. Much must be done to assure that, at
least, the situation grows no worse.

The United Nations is essential. The Charter and the machinery
which it established must be maintained in full vigor; the voice of
the General Assembly against the use of force must remain clear
and firm. The presence of the UN should be invoked where it is
likely to be effective to prevent or allay crises. The channels of
communication between nations through diplomatic missions,

through their missions at the UN Headquarters and delegations to UN Assemblies, must be kept open and functioning. They permit continual negotiations which are the basic means for making it possible for nations to settle differences without force, as the UN Charter requires. The conciliatory and mediatory opportunities for governments, for officials of governments, for leading citizens, for officials of the United Nations and particularly for the Secretary-General must be developed and enhanced. In these efforts there is use for the methods of the law and the skills of the lawyers—in negotiating, in developing, expressing and confirming areas of agreement, in evolving the institutional possibilities inherent in a document like the UN Charter; for example, the ascendancy of the General Assembly, the establishment of the United Nations Emergency Force, the stand-by planning of the Collective Measures Committee. Against a later day, too, particularly as it relates to the possibility of substantial control of armaments, there is a need for additional studies similar to the one conducted by the Carnegie Endowment for International Peace relative to an international police force.

3

If there is now a clear coincidence of interest for all nations to avoid major force, it is also in their interest to make it less likely that force will be used, intentionally or accidentally. The United States, the USSR and other leading countries must themselves refrain from initiating the use of force and exert every influence on all others also to refrain. All nations have an important interest to assure that no single nation anywhere will initiate the use of force against another.

Recognition by both sides in the global conflict that they must avoid force requires also that they recognize that any changes from the *status quo* must be pursuant to peaceful agreement. In some areas bristling with tension, conflicting interests may not at present permit any substantial changes by peaceful agreement. But force must be avoided, and the incitements and temptations to use force. Thus, for a current example, the Soviet Union must appreciate the circumstances which render it impossible for the West to abandon West Berlin, and which would compel the West to meet forcibly any serious jeopardy to their presence there. Subject to that limitation there may be room for some agreed peaceful change in the status of Berlin, in the presence of Western forces, in access between West Berlin and West Germany. It may be possible—again there will be call on the ingenuity of the law and of lawyers—to substitute a permanent peaceful status for the city for the present occupation status; and the likelihood of agreement may be enhanced by the symbolic, political, administrative role of the UN, or by its presence.

Despite continued failure and frustration, there is also some real coincidence of interest in efforts to control armaments, to give confidence if not assurance that nations which do not yet have them do not acquire weapons of mass destruction, and that nations which do have them will not use them. There must be intensified search, in particular, for agreement on measures to assure that there will be no surprise attack and no accidental war. There is coincidence of interest too in efforts to moderate the frantic race for new weapons of incalculable destructive power. Reliable agreements, however small and preliminary in character, can break the cycle in which tensions lead to more arms and arms increase tensions. If in a world without trust, such agreements require reliability and confidence, both sides may have to pay a price in submitting to essential verifications and inspections. Both sides must earnestly consider that there may be more security for them in known controls on armaments than in the fearful uncertainties of unbridled competition in the armaments of the future.

Areas emerging into international awareness may develop new conflicts of interest and new tensions, but nations may also be persuaded that it would be preferable for all if these areas were isolated from conflict. Agreement by the United States and the Soviet Union on the nonmilitarization of Antarctica is a small example, and an augury of hope.

The development of uses of outer space seems to offer another such opportunity. The potentialities of these uses for mutual destruction are terrifying in their uncertainty; the United States and the USSR might well consider whether it would not be preferable for both to eliminate the risks by agreement that outer space will not be used for launching weapons of destruction. The potentialities, on the other hand, of these uses of outer space for revolutionary benefits to all suggest also a coincidence of interest in cooperation for peaceful development and use. Here again, essential verifications and inspections will be necessary.

Allowing for many differences, there is reminder, if not analogy, in the early state of atomic energy, say in 1945. The tragic failure of attempts to "demilitarize" the atom and to arrange for cooperation in its peaceful exploitation must not be repeated. There is hope that the lessons of that failure, as well as the difference in the two situations, may help avoid a new failure. There is not, as there was in the case of the atom, a monopoly on one side, and a consequent fear that controls would freeze the other in a state of permanent inferiority. There has not yet been sufficient progress on either side to warrant a feeling that controls would involve a sacrifice of advantage. There can be no confidence on either side that, in the long run, a race into use of outer space for weapons would enhance its military superiority or security. It may again be difficult to persuade either side that a monopoly in an international development agency would work; but it should be possible to persuade both sides that exchange of information, "traffic" rules and controls, and joint ventures are indeed in the interest of both nations, and all nations. There can be new law here—new standards of conduct, new institutions, new procedures. And lawyers can make their contribution here as they did in the Acheson-Lilienthal Report on controlling the atom, and in subsequent, partly successful attempts to achieve cooperation on peaceful uses of atomic energy.

4

After World War II the United States was a leading proponent of further development of international law and institutions. The Soviet Union, by comparison, was recalcitrant and reactionary. Under pressure of the tensions of the East-West conflict, however, the United States too has receded into attitudes far less cooperative, if not isolationist. The barely-escaped Bricker Amendments; the genocide convention buried in the Senate; the indifferent participation in the activities of the International Law Commission and of the Sixth Committee of the General Assembly; the negative attitude of the United States toward adjudication by the International Court of Justice; the abandonment and avoidance of efforts to establish common international standards by multilateral agreement, such as the draft covenant on human rights —these are but examples. Even in established areas of international law, there has been a tendency to deal with issues as problems in American foreign policy, to be determined unilaterally by the United States in the light of immediate United States interests, rather than with a sense of obligation by Congress, the Executive, or the courts to abide by rules of international law or the provisions of a treaty.

If the United States record has not been brilliant, particularly in regard to the further development of international law, the United States has in fact largely abided by international law. The record of the Soviet Union has been deplorable. Although the Soviet Union has not flatly rejected international law as a capitalist invention, it has not given other nations much reason to hope that it would abide by accepted international law even in normal circumstances, or cooperate in the development of further rules in the common interest.

In practice both sides have tacitly observed many of the principles and practices of international law and comity, and even the Soviet Union has, for the most part, avoided overt and flagrant violations. There is also a new, particular hope that both the United States and the Soviet Union may yet recognize an identity of interest in maintaining and promoting international law. For international law may be the bridge between each of the big contenders and the emerging new nations. In the keen competition between East and West for the favor of the neutral, uncommitted, and developing nations, both sides may find that the body of international law serves to afford to the new nations a sense of equality, dignity, and sovereign independence. If international law rarely calls for explicit application in regard to issues between the United States and the Soviet Union, each of them may find it advisable to apply international law in relations with Ghana or Morocco. In the bipolar world there is, consequently, a new opportunity for "horizontal" development of international law, for its maintenance and extension to the new nations. If this occurs, international law may be generally strengthened and have greater effect even in its application between the two camps.

The "vertical" growth of international law, the development of new aids to order, is more difficult in a world so sharply divided, but not impossible. If the Soviet Union is not eager to cooperate, other nations can still build law at least for areas which are not the battlefield of the big conflict. And the pressure of the new nations may compel cooperation even from the Soviet Union. As to how to build such law, there are differences of opinion as to whether international law can grow and strengthen better by the process of codification and "legislation," or by a natural, "common law" growth of practice and custom. While the latter may offer more promise, some codification, in selected areas ripe for it, might at least have educational value.

But if the main reliance for growth is to be on practice and custom, it is important that such practice and custom be collected and made available, and perhaps restated from time to time. Today it is difficult if not impossible to learn what nations are in fact doing, what are their customs and practices in international relations. A body like the UN, with special financial assistance from governmental or private sources, should undertake to learn, collect, systematize, and make generally available the practices of the political and judicial organs of governments, as well as those of arbitral and similar bodies dealing with matters of international or transnational concern. Worthy individual contributions to this end have already been initiated: there are Professor E. Lauterpacht's summaries of practice in the United Kingdom; similar materials on the United States have begun to appear in the pages of the *American Journal of International Law*; efforts of this kind are beginning also in India and promised in Australia. Also, the State Department is engaged in bringing up to date Hackworth's *Digest of International Law*, and it is reported that similar works have been initiated in the United Kingdom, in France, and in Switzerland.

5

An urgent need, even in a bipolar world, is the development of legal "substitutes for war." The United Nations Charter outlaws the use of force except in defense against armed attack. In fact, with exceptions noted, nationals have abstained from using force in the past when force may have been justified under international law. The result has been to leave areas of international interest unprotected. There have developed no clear agreed standards of conduct, nor any clear, agreed, and effective procedure for handling those situations which in the past were dealt with by force. It is not yet clear what should happen if one nation repeatedly ·violates the territorial integrity of another, if nations do not meet their financial or other contractual or treaty obligations to other nations, if they mistreat the nationals of other nations, if they endanger important economic interests of other nations or of their nationals, if they defame or deceive them, if they interfere with their communications. Rights of flight over the territory of other nations at various heights are matters in dispute and sources of tension, as is the right to use international waterways which are under national control. And the national treatment of human beings and of their fundamental rights continues to evoke the concern of other nations, while the acting states continue to insist that such matters are entirely domestic and of no international concern.

If, in regard to these and other problems, force continues in fact to be avoided, tensions will remain and fester. (It would not seem desirable to bring every such instance to the General Assembly for *ad hoc* political consideration, especially since there are really no principles of conduct to guide the Assembly.) Ultimately, then, if the rules against self-help by force are to survive, it is important that standards of conduct and machinery for settling disputes develop quickly—particularly for areas involving important interests which nations might be tempted again to "vindicate" by force. Such developments are more difficult, but some growth appears possible, even in the shadow of the Cold War.

More work is needed to identify the areas and problems to which this concern is particularly applicable, to analyze the competing interests, to set forth or develop equitable standards of conduct, to examine existing procedures, and, if necessary, develop new ones appropriate for the settlement of disputes. It will be necessary to reexamine hitherto accepted ideas of the respective areas of domestic interest and of international concern, and relate them to a world in which many "domestic" matters arouse keen international concern. "Domestic" transactions often have transnational character. Foreign and international acts often have profound impact on the "domestic" life of nations. It will be necessary to achieve—by agreement, or by the growth of custom—rules of conduct, as well as procedures for applying them. It is hardly necessary, of course, to develop rules or even identical machinery and procedures for different problems.

In the long run, a strong deterrent to disorder in international affairs lies in the patterns and habits of peaceful intercourse which contribute to order in all nations. Among such institutions in existence are, obviously, the international postal and telecommunications systems. But the daily details of increasing transnational and international relations promise another contribution to order and an important opportunity to law and lawyers. The development, for example, of standard commercial practices, of common "forms" for contracts, bills, and notes, transcends competing ideological and political and security interests, and helps establish a common framework within which tensions recede and order grows. It is desirable to promote uniform or corresponding practices in these and related fields, in direct negotiations through private groups, and through such bodies as the Economic Commission for Europe.

Areas of a different kind also offer some possibilities for increasing order. Meetings of scientists, even in the delicate field of arms control, have proved fruitful. Scientific cooperation in other fields —the International Geophysical Year and the International Committee on Space Research—warrants encouragement for similar endeavors. The artistic and intellectual communities also have proved that they afford opportunities for building up cooperative exchange, and helping create a more open society even behind the Iron Curtain. "Opening up" of the Soviet Union could be a result of, as well as a contribution to, the strengthening of international order.

To some the goal devoutly to be wished is the submission of all disputes and differences between the United States and the Soviet Union to the International Court of Justice. It is common knowledge, however, that the Soviet Union has never used the International Court and that the United States is not overeager to submit to its jurisdiction. Much study and effort have been devoted to developing the Court and other machinery for adjudicating disputes so that they might "work" even between the United States and the Soviet Union. But the weakness is not in existing machinery for adjudication, and it cannot be cured by improving the machinery. There is no agreement between East and West on standards of conduct, and therefore no basis for decisions as to whether any given standards have been observed or violated. There is no agreement between them to submit to a process of adjudication. And the Soviet Union in particular generally rejects the notion basic to adjudication: that any court can be impartial.

It would no doubt be desirable if the United States and the Soviet Union were to submit broadly to the jurisdiction of the Court. The proposal made by a United States spokesman to add a clause to this effect to new treaties which both the United States and the Soviet Union would ratify has something to commend it, in principle; compulsory submission to the jurisdiction of the Court is in fact a common provision in recent treaties. But to be effective there must first be the substantive agreements, and these have been lacking. Indeed the addition of this clause to an agreement might even render it less likely that the Soviet Union would adhere to the agreement. United States insistence upon such a clause in any agreement might be viewed by the Russians, who do not consider the International Court of Justice "impartial," as an effort to load the scales of the agreement against the Russians.

One cannot, then, be optimistic for the future of any adjudicating process for settling disputes or relaxing tensions between East and West. But courts, we have suggested, are not the only "legal" machinery, and in international affairs today may not even be the most promising. In time of tension between big powers, representing a desire for change by at least one of them, courts tend to be an unacceptable preserver of the *status quo*. They are to be used for important matters; if used they are to be obeyed. If not obeyed, courts may be destroyed. Particularly in situations of tension, other forms of resolution promise better.

There are, of course, the organs of the UN, which may be used at least to confirm a resolution of a dispute if not to bring it about. There are mediatory, conciliatory, "good offices" bodies in the UN and outside it. Most important, there are the lines of direct communication, at embassies, in third countries, in the corridors of the UN—at summit level or working levels—which must be maintained as ultimately the best hope for resolving issues and relaxing tensions. For all "legal" disputes between any nations are also political disputes. Between East and West, where there exist few admitted rules of law and no agreed tribunal to apply them, all disputes are basically political to be resolved through political institutions, primarily by direct contact.

Special machinery, fundamentally political in character, may be created. Some existed and worked when both sides wished it to work, as in Germany and Austria. In Korea an armistice was ultimately negotiated. In each case it was machinery basically bilateral, a body which did not strive for impartial adjudication (which the Soviet Union, we repeat, has not been ready to accept) but a bilateral body for hard, patient negotiation. The creation of such bodies, generally of equal representation, for *ad hoc* negotiations or perhaps for continuing general contact and discussion, still appears to offer the best hope for relaxing tensions between the East and West. This too is order, and law, and here also the lawyer needs to lend his gifts for planning, building, developing, and administering institutions and procedures.

6

World tensions result not only from the way the big powers glare at each other, but from the quickening explosions of new nationalisms, the demand of dependent peoples for independence and a greater share of the world's wealth. The recent and contemporary history has given new vitality to the "principle of equal rights and self-determination" recognized in the United Nations Charter, although it remains for the lawyers of all nations to consider to what extent this has now become a juridical principle in the law of nations.

Basically, the new nations have set themselves three tremendous tasks: to establish a nation out of heterogeneous groups; to build this nation with meager resources, only a fraction per capita of what developing European nations (for example, Germany, Italy) had in the nineteenth century; to give their people the advantages of a welfare state. The older nations must take account of these gigantic undertakings in their relations with these nations.

The importance of the economic growth of the new nations for the reduction of tensions, and specific programs for assistance to these nations, for cooperative economic development on a bilateral basis or through the UN and other multilateral agencies, are discussed in Chapter 3 of this book. The machinery and procedures for economic development there suggested are, of course, political and legal institutions also. Ultimately, it is necessary for the lawyer to join the economists and others to fashion arrangements whereby the resources of the older, more developed countries are in fact made available to the newer and poorer countries. There may be need to create, or modify, or develop new international institutions and procedures. There may be need for the lawyer to help accommodate conflicting national legislation, including tax regimes and monetary regulation.

Here, we would speak also of the relation to the new nations of other aspects of "law." The new nations are, of course, members of the UN and of many specialized agencies, and are already making their voices heard there. They have entered into international relations in accordance with international practice. But there are other areas where law and legal institutions can contribute to the healthy growth of these nations and of their relations to the older nations. To suggest that there may be reexamination is not to urge rejection or to assume even that there will or ought to be important modification. Examination may well show that traditional international law was not a law for the powerful few in a private club of nations, but in fact provides basic accommodations, all generally applicable today in a society of sovereign nations.

In any event, some standards must be agreed upon and accepted. In specific areas the new nations eager for assistance from more developed nations in their struggle to preserve their independence, to develop their resources, to raise their standards of life, will have to recognize and respect the interests of those whose assistance they seek. There will have to be agreement, for example, on the rights of foreign investors, on the status of persons engaged in technical assistance to them, as well as general confidence that the new nations will abide by their agreements and by diplomatic immunities and amenities.

In their integration into an international community with even an imperfect rule of law, the new nations such as those in Africa will need sympathetic assistance. They begin "from scratch" and must come far even to begin to live by the present state of international law. There is need to assist them in their education in international matters, to help them to apply to their own situation the international law and practice of older nations, to train their lawyers and diplomats.

The task is not made easier by the comparatively primitive state of their domestic institutions; by their poverty and large illiterate populations; by differences among the African nations themselves, including differences of language and mores which render difficult even regional grouping and federation. They will have to look to leadership within their own groups. Free nations elsewhere will have to earn leadership by exemplary adherence to the rules of good international behavior in accordance with law.

There is urgent need to train young leaders of these new nations in the traditions of democracy and representative government, of individual freedoms and rights under law, modified as need be to meet local needs and mores. The United States and its Western allies, in particular, should invite representatives from these nations to see and to study; they should be prepared also to welcome students to Western institutions, as well as to send teachers and other experts to advise on the establishment and growth of political institutions, the promulgation of constitutions, the training and selection of judges, the creation of a Bar of responsibility and leadership.

7

The nations of the West and other nations with free institutions, similar traditions, and generally common political interests undoubtedly have developed, among themselves, the most advanced legal and political institutions and the greatest willingness to submit to the rule of law, even to the adjudicatory process. It is among these nations in particular—or among regionally associated groups of them—that we may look for new international law, new substantive agreements of a bilateral or a multilateral character, greater acceptance of mediation, arbitration, and adjudication, and a heartening habit of settling disputes and relaxing tensions by the process of negotiation. If where tensions exist all questions tend to become political, as tensions recede political questions can be rendered "legal," to be decided by tribunals in accordance with agreed standards. Further progress in the rule of law within this group will, of course, minimize tensions among the nations in the group— and also make it less likely that "internecine" differences will be exploited by the Soviet Union.

It will provide, also, a focus and an example for other nations to follow and to join. Immediately, even nations not as close to each other as those of the West may be prepared to accept "rule of law" for particular problems. Consequently, even nations with some hostility between them can better accept the results of an adjudication or some other form of impartial decision or recommendation rather than try to achieve the same result by compromise in negotiations. (In some areas a small group—perhaps the

United States, the United Kingdom and Canada—could establish among themselves a near-"perfect" rule of law as an example to the nations. This might be achieved without incurring the dangers of "fragmentation," of new divisions within this rule-of-law bloc, which argue against some other types of regional groupings.)

There is no doubt that within this rule-of-law community there could be more use of the International Court of Justice, at least on issues not of vital moment. Among these nations, it should be possible to establish that using the Court is not a hostile act. The Court would be used and its judgments respected; successful use of the Court contributing to its growth.

In this connection the United States has hardly shown a good example. Current efforts to repeal the Connally Amendment have been unsuccessful to date; this reservation has not even been abolished as between the United States and selected friendly nations.

The Connally Amendment reserves to the United States the right to determine finally that a matter is essentially within the domestic jurisdiction of the United States, and therefore not an international dispute subject to the jurisdiction of the International Court. This raises the most difficult question of all, a question that lies at the root of all efforts to develop law and order: What is essentially a domestic matter which nations are free to decide as they see the right, and what, on the other hand, is a matter of legitimate concern to other nations as to which other nations may properly make representations, seek UN consideration, or even international adjudication?

Article 2(7) of the UN Charter, which provides that the UN is not authorized "to intervene in matters which are essentially within the domestic jurisdiction of any state," has raised as many difficult political and judicial questions as any other provision in the Charter. The United States has generally taken the view that the "domestic jurisdiction" clause does not bar discussion in the General Assembly of matters which concern other nations.

Surely nothing can be "essentially domestic" and barred to the United Nations if it becomes a threat to international peace and security.

There are equally great difficulties presented by "domestic jurisdiction" as a bar to the jurisdiction of the International Court of Justice. Presumably the Court will have to take into account developments in international law in determining whether a matter is proper for international adjudication or is the private affair of the acting State. Presumably, the International Court of Justice, a conservative institution as all courts tend to be, will not be the first to see radical growth in international law. Even if there are very few questions, even "domestic" ones, that can be barred from discussion in the UN's General Assembly, it does not follow that the Court will lightly extend the jurisdiction optionally given to it by the nations to areas traditionally "domestic." Surely, the fact that there may be questions about which another nation is in controversy with the United States will not *ipso facto* render it "nondomestic" to the United States and therefore justiciable by the Court.

In any event whether a matter is justiciable or not is clearly a question about the jurisdiction of the Court which should not be decided by a party to a dispute. The reservation is therefore improper in principle. Because of the applicable rule of reciprocity, it has also hurt the United States by giving the same power to deny the jurisdiction of the Court to any State whom the United States might wish to sue.

What is most unfortunate about the Connally Amendment is the appearance of isolationism, of refusal to submit to the jurisdiction of the Court even vis-à-vis its friends on a reciprocal basis. Even without this reservation there would be few cases in which the United States could be brought to the Court against its will; there are not many causes of action justiciable in the Court, and there have been few cases in which the United States has in fact been sued. Most of the few suits which might arise against the

United States would probably arise out of treaties which provide for compulsory Court jurisdiction and to which the Connally Amendment would not apply. On the other hand, even with this reservation, it should be obvious that the United States, through the Executive Branch, cannot properly invoke this reservation in circumstances where the matter at issue is patently not domestic but a legitimate matter of concern to another nation. The reservation then will not properly allow the United States to deny to the Court jurisdiction in the large majority of those disputes which might come to it. Even in the rare instance where invoking the reservation might be proper, the Executive Branch might well and properly decide not to invoke it because of the unfortunate consequences for the United States in world opinion. Finally, where the United States honestly believes that the matter may truly be domestic, it might better, as has been suggested, submit that question for a preliminary opinion by the Court.

The reservation then is not of great import to the United States. Withdrawing it would not increase substantially the extent to which the United States is subject to the Court, but would remove a continuous reminder of United States' reluctance to submit to international adjudication. The reservation gives constant lie to our professions of support for the rule of law, and opens to charges of hypocrisy United States criticism of the Soviet Union for its unwillingness to submit to law. Failure to remove the reservation after the recent attempt to do so would only emphasize and aggravate the fault of the United States in the eyes of the world. We may hope that the failure is only a brief delay.

8

In a world of pervasive malaise and disorder the perfect "rule of law" seems remote. Treaties with ideal provisions will not be signed; courts with extensive jurisdiction over all nations and issues will not be used or obeyed, even if created. Efforts directed toward optimum solutions have their principal justification only in hope that they can be soon achieved. Fortunately for mankind, it is in the interest of all, including the Big Powers:

To avoid the use of force themselves and to exert every influence against international use of force by any nation anywhere;

To maintain the United Nations which, among other things, helps preserve the balance between East and West and serves as a bridge to the new nations;

To seek their military security through reliable, reciprocal control of armaments rather than to risk the uncertain consequences and dangers of an unbridled arms race and the ever-present danger of sudden war, accidental or deliberate;

To bar the use of outer space for weapons of destruction and to cooperate in the exploration and use of outer space for beneficial peaceful purposes;

To respect and develop international law, particularly as a common bridge to the new nations;

To develop practices and procedures as "substitutes for war" to deal with situations which in the past may have evoked the use or threat of force;

To promote cooperation and common practices and forms in the daily commerce of nations, among businessmen, scientists, artists, others; and

To keep open and to increase channels of direct communication between all nations, particularly between East and West, as the best forum for settling disputes that may arise as well as for relaxing or preventing tensions.

For the new nations the old must show sympathy and understanding, not only by assisting them in economic ways but by helping to invent useful legal and political institutions. Old and new nations must reason together about maintaining and improving the law of nations. The old must help the new to achieve at least present levels of international law and order, and to establish free institutions and freedom under law for their citizens.

The old free nations of the West with common values and traditions have even greater opportunities. Among them there can be important developments in international law, and substantial growth of international institutions, including the International Court of Justice and other adjudicatory bodies, as an example to the world. The United States must regain its leadership in this group by regaining attitudes of cooperation and submission to law at least vis-à-vis its friends; it can begin clearing its skirts by revoking the Connally Reservation.

Throughout, the responsible role for law and lawyers is clear. They can help develop the possibilities of existing institutions like the UN and help build new institutions and administer them when they are built. Individually, as citizens and leaders, and in their association, they can help meet the challenge presented by the needs of new nations, assist them in developing their domestic institutions, in moving toward regional cooperation, and toward a life under law in the community of nations. Programs for bringing students and sending teachers are an obvious need; an undertaking—say by the American Bar Association—to send books and documents of legal and political import would make an important contribution.

Lawyers have no magic formula for bringing peace and ease among nations. The specific programs suggested—development of legal "substitutes for force," the study of the assumptions of international law, the collection and dissemination of the facts of international practice, and new manifestations of support for the rule of law among the free nations,—are indeed modest. But of such is the kingdom of law in the real world. The hope for relaxing tensions lies in the gradual recognition, especially by the Big Powers, that there are in fact substantial and important areas of common interest among them—and there is consequently a place for law as well as politics.

The new atomic age demands new thinking to produce some bold imaginative plan to get us out of the present dreary and dangerous impasse.

—LORD BOYD-ORR

3

AGENDA FOR ECONOMIC DEVELOPMENT

Harlan Cleveland and Irving Swerdlow

The revolutionary tendencies toward land reform and higher real wages, the desire to eliminate individuals or classes which are deemed to stand in the way of higher morale for more people, the attempt to produce even by violence the greatest good for the greatest number—these are the tension-producing attitudes of our time.

They are "good" tensions in that they correctly express man's hopes for more welfare, equity, achievement, and participation. But there are other tensions which result from (*a*) maneuvers by powerful countries to use economic development programs as a means for gaining tactical advantages in a "Cold War" struggle between rival philosophies, and (*b*) efforts by extremist politicians within the less developed countries to exploit men's hopes as a source of political power in ways that retard rather than speed the process of economic development.

For the relatively richer countries of the West, the cue is not to complain loudly and ineffectually about such perversions, but to get on with the task of helping the poorer countries take advantage of their opportunities. If we keep our eyes on this objective,

43

the "bad" tensions can be reduced in at least three ways by the vigorous promotion of economic growth:

• Both Soviet policy and extreme nationalism in the less developed areas feed on the feeling of inferiority and consequent resentment of Western power that is an unforgotten legacy of the period of colonial rule and business exploitation. Visible signs of economic improvement help overcome these feelings on the part of the less developed countries.

• Rapid economic development provides a focus of political attention in each country on its own affairs, and discourages international comparisons. Even rapid growth in the poor countries may not narrow the absolute gap in standards between rich nations and poor, for the rich nations are developing too. But, as indicated above, the morale of individuals and groups is not a matter of absolute standards; it is a feeling that is relative to time, place, and circumstance. People in poor countries who see their own institutions developing in such a way as to provide a growing measure of welfare ("standard of living," only very roughly measurable by per capita Gross National Product), a less and less inequitable treatment of the more numerous poor, a sense of achievement both in these material terms and in respectability and "acceptance," and a sense of participation in the process of governance by which these things are being brought about—such people are less likely to threaten their rising morale by roaming the streets in violent mobs seeking a panacea for the problems that still remain unsolved. From the point of view of poor people in poor countries, the most obvious gap to be narrowed is not the one that separates their per capita GNP from that of the United States or Western Europe, but the gap between their own poverty and the standards already enjoyed by the rich and powerful in their own countries.

• Economic development creates relevant and interesting tasks for élite groups in the less developed countries. The processes of economic growth, and the accompanying tasks of social institution-building, make necessary the development of a "modern" leadership which can fill the vacuum created by the erosion of traditional power structures. Quite apart from its intrinsic purpose, economic development provides a sense of achievement in relation to worth-while goals that are urgent and exciting for the growing number of educated people who have come to believe, not without reason, that higher education should make possible higher living standards and more political independence.

2

The economic development of the poorer countries will be a function both of the actions they themselves take or make possible and of the cooperative arrangements the richer countries make to participate in these actions. In order to move toward "modernization," the dominant political and executive leadership in the poorer countries generally have to:

1. Accept the fact that the achievement of a satisfactory rate of economic growth largely depends on their own efforts. They will have to supply most of the capital, skilled labor, and management from their own resources. Foreign assistance, important and necessary as it is, is of marginal magnitude compared to total requirements.

2. Accept the fact that it will take a long time to achieve a satisfactory level of consumption. Resource growth must be allocated between consumption and savings in a manner designed to stimulate further economic growth, and it is necessary to minimize any political advantages in advocating too hasty an increase in consumption.

3. Develop institutions and value standards that are consistent with economic growth. These include the ability and willingness of governments to make necessary resource allocations, and attitudes appropriate to development administration. More fundamentally, these include the development among enough people of the capacity and urge for "creativity," the zest for adaptation and innovation

that makes possible self-generated economic growth. Further, these may include, where necessary, adjustments in values and institutions to meet rapid increases in population that threaten to overwhelm the capacity for increase in capital.

4. Develop the channels of information and communication, supported by a rising level of education and technical training, that seem to be everywhere a basis for economically advanced societies. The increased ability to communicate is clearly associated with modernization; without it, the market economy based on specialization and trade becomes impossible to attain.

These essential requirements for economic growth are not easily met, for most of the new nations lack the leadership with the necessary technical and managerial knowledge and experience. Consequently the high-income countries are already, and will increasingly be, providing from the outside not only part of the needed financial resources but also a part of the high-level human resources of the poorer countries. Just when the world contains more "independent" nations than ever before, the dynamics of technical aid and cross-cultural institution-building make intimate interdependence the natural order of international affairs.

For the high-income countries, the new work of building the institutions of modernization inside the poor countries has several aspects, which are treated at some length in the remainder of this chapter. In summary, the rich countries must face the moral and political issues involved by:

1. Adjusting their economic and political policies to lend a more urgent priority to rapid economic development. Helping the poor countries achieve a satisfactory rate of growth is probably the most important and almost certainly the most complex problem now facing the richer countries. The latter need to face the long-term commitment and the degree of cross-cultural intervention that are necessarily involved. And since the distinction between their "domestic" and their "foreign" affairs has been irrevocably blurred by technological and political interdependence, the richer

countries must also be willing to think of all "domestic" policies as partly international in scope.

2. Improving both national and international institutions that serve as a bridge between richer and poorer countries in the field of economic development. These include more effective international organizations for promoting economic development; a better system for concentrating the resources from all the UN agencies on the development problem of a single nation; more support for multilateral regional approaches to economic development; a policy that enables the richer countries to contribute to change-inducing programs in the poor countries and avoid the appearance of merely supporting existing régimes.

3. Providing more resources, both real wealth and personnel, to help the poorer countries in their efforts to achieve economic growth. This is not just a matter of the total volume of investment, but of management and administrative skills, the special costs of preinvestment planning, and the knotty problem of agricultural surpluses.

The list of actions that can provide the impetus of an adequate rate of economic development is long, if somewhat shopworn. Many are now parts of government programs, and all of them have at some time or other been proposed for governmental action. What is needed is a more imaginative execution of these more or less accepted programs, more vigorously administered and more adequately financed.

As Americans we cannot but be especially conscious of the bottlenecks that result from inaction or inadequate action by the richer countries. It is these which are stressed in the pages that follow. But it is worth repeating that rapid development, above all, requires of the leadership of the low-income countries the attitudes and actions indicated above. There are far more instances of inadequate growth owing to a lack of vigorous leadership and incapacity in the underdeveloped countries than those resulting from insufficient support from high-income countries.

3

In Europe, the movement toward economic integration reflects the recognition that nationalism in its traditional forms is not fit for modern states. But fit or not, nationalism is still, perhaps more than ever, the world's most influential political idea. Nationalism is often a reaction against a status of inferiority and an urge toward self-respect, power over and control of one's own destiny. It can be a creative, dynamic force, cementing together a people and enabling them to achieve a unity of purpose and action which would be impossible without it, or it can be negative, disruptive, and divisive.

In the newly independent or emerging countries, the appeal of nationalism has usually been exploited by political leaders to help create the country, and all leaders, all classes, all vested interest groups must claim to be its true interpreters.

Coupled with this intense nationalism is often a profound desire for something called "neutrality" or "nonalignment," which means staying out of the ideological crossfire between the West and the Soviet bloc. This desire may be the result of precarious geographical location, political detachment, economic self-absorption, a yen for feeling self-identity, or some combination of these.

These feelings are so strong and so pervasive that the richer countries in the Free World must necessarily find ways to support rather than oppose them—even though we know that the mutual involvement of the nations in each other's internal affairs has made neutralism a difficult policy to pursue for long, and we suspect that nationalism does not represent the final stage in mankind's search for viable political institutions.

A recognition of the force of nationalism calls for an attitude of understanding that is sometimes not easy to establish or maintain. When hurried land reform programs impinge on the rights of foreigners, when foreign investments are expropriated without compensation, when appeals for popular support are based on violent antiforeign feelings, it is difficult to continue pressing for constructive programs that encourage trade, provide more investment funds, and strengthen the machinery to improve international relations. Yet, if economic development is to achieve the direction and substance needed, the policies and actions of the countries concerned must be directed toward making nationalism a constructive force in economic development.

Similarly, the "nonalignment" policies of many areas must not be treated as barriers to the flow of international assistance. To tie support for economic development to alliance policy has proved to be ineffectual; to stigmatize neutrality as immoral is merely offensive. In any case, the friendly government that compromises its nonalignment with a reluctant alliance can be readily overthrown on the very issue of too close association with either one of the military blocs.

There are, moreover, positive advantages in the nonalignment of new nations which are unlikely in any case to be important factors in the equation of military power. The existence of a sizable uncommitted group of nations can serve as a powerful force in reducing international tensions. The existence of neutral nations reduces the area where the forces of both sides physically confront each other, which is always an explosive situation. These uncommitted nations are also a force for moderation, by compelling the two conflicting sides to appraise the likely impact of their future policies on the neutrals. Where there are only the effects on the enemy camp to be considered, the Cold War undoubtedly becomes fiercer and the possibility of serious incident greater.

The recommended policy, that we should be relaxed and friendly about nationalism and nonalignment, has important implications for the management of the flow of technical aid and investment to the less developed areas of the Free World. It argues that to the greatest possible extent such input should be directed through multilateral organizations *in which the less developed countries themselves participate.* The leader of a newly independent country will hardly relish the role of supplicant rather than participant in dealing with a cartel of aid-givers and lenders.

4

As the Western countries move into high gear in their assistance to economic development in Asia, Africa, and Latin America, it is well to face frankly the fact that, so far, the international rivalry between the Soviet bloc and the Western democracies has probably been of benefit to some of the less developed countries. However much we may deplore the competitive aspects, there is no doubt that the Soviet policy of technical aid and public investment after 1954 was sparked by the popularity of Point Four, the UN technical assistance programs, the World Bank's activity, and other smaller national initiatives by England, Germany, and Japan. In turn, the Soviet competition has intensified the sense of urgency in the Western countries, and has persuaded reluctant legislatures to put up larger amounts of aid than might otherwise have been available during the 1950's. The problem for the 1960's is to fashion aid programs that focus on the kinds of economic growth desired and the kinds of institutions to be built in the less developed areas, rather than on competitive short-term political "impact."

Soviet bloc economic activity has taken the form of an increase in trade and credits to the underdeveloped countries. The over-all magnitudes are still not large compared with those of the Western world. Total Soviet bloc nonmilitary loan commitments made to eighteen underdeveloped countries with which aid agreements had been signed amounted by the end of 1959 to about $2.5 billion, of which only $550 million had actually been drawn by that date. During this same period, United States aid to these eighteen countries was $4.3 billion, and the United States has extended a total of $19 billion to fifty-five underdeveloped countries. Also by comparison, the World Bank, in the decade 1949 to 1959 had loaned over $4 billion in development loans and dispersed nearly $3 billion. However, such success as the USSR has enjoyed has been due to factors other than mere magnitude. Soviet trade and lending has been concentrated in relatively few countries, and in the smaller of them the absolute magnitudes loom relatively large.

The program has been managed with considerable flexibility, and quick advantage has been taken of difficulties that have arisen between the United States and other countries. The novelty of the program contributed to the wide publicity it received, and in the early stages there was not time for the inevitable conflicts to arise. Now, as the program has rolled on, the benefits of novelty have been falling away, and the Soviets have been increasingly involved in the familiar irritations of conducting a foreign aid program. There is evidence that the Soviets have made most of the major errors that characterized the experimental days of United States bilateral aid (such as overconcentration on short-term "impact" and overenthusiasm for "monuments") in roughly the same order that the United States made them four or five years earlier.

Since the launching of the post-Stalin policy in 1954, three of the largest recipients of Soviet loans have found themselves on worsened terms with the Soviet bloc (Yugoslavia, Egypt, and India), and the most dramatic Soviet success was scored in a country that had at that time received no Soviet economic aid (Iraq). We need not fall into the error of ascribing to Soviet economic policy all the successes that ought properly to be ascribed to broader political factors—or of believing that the Soviets can somehow make more political capital out of economic aid than can the United States or other Western countries.

A more significant effect of the new Soviet policy is that countries heavily dependent upon Soviet trade or loans may be subjected to irresistible pressure to adopt policies insisted upon by the USSR. The single important case in which this has been tried is Yugoslavia, and the result is of great significance: the Yugoslavs chose to go without the Soviet loans, at great economic cost to themselves, rather than knuckle under to Soviet, and in some degree Chinese, pressures. A Western policy of hostility toward countries that accept Soviet loans and trade offers might weaken their ability to resist Soviet pressure. The intense spirit of nationalism in the newly independent countries is their greatest defense against victimization by Soviet economic pressure. But the Free World can assist them in resisting Soviet interference by participating in their economic growth whether or not the Communists are also doing so—and by standing ready to ease the economic blows of any withdrawal of Soviet trade or loans.

The reaction of the high-income countries of the Free World to the expansion of the Communist bloc "aid and trade" program has been a mixture of resentment and futility; short-sighted resentment at the underdeveloped areas for accepting this aid and futility in the efforts to curtail it and expose its potential dangers. Most of the underdeveloped countries are so anxious for additional capital resources and technical assistance, so wary of becoming too identified with only one side of the foreign conflict, that Soviet aid is acceptable even though most responsible leaders in the countries involved are aware of the political pressures it may bring in its train. Efforts by the high-income countries to outbid the Communist bloc aid only emphasize the advantages to the underdeveloped countries of encouraging this form of competition.

A change of policy that invites and encourages Communist bloc countries to participate in multilateral arrangements for providing additional capital and technical assistance to underdeveloped countries can have important, worth-while results. This includes new invitations to join the World Bank (IBRD) and the International Monetary Fund, which the Communist bloc has thus far avoided.

It seems unlikely that Russia and other Communist bloc countries would take part in such multilateral organizations, even if they were invited to do so, since it would require their making large contributions to programs they could not hope to control. They would probably prefer to remain free to use most of their resources on a bilateral basis, as the United States now does. But their added participation in multilateral agencies should be welcomed. If both they and the richer countries of the Free World make more use of multilateral agencies the effect would be to subject a larger share of Soviet foreign economic activity to international control under the preponderant influence of non-Communist countries.

5

The focus on internal development tends to obscure the fact that international trade is at the center of world economic growth, particularly in the underdeveloped countries. Most of these countries have economies heavily dependent on the export of a relatively few primary commodities, such as rubber, tea, tin, rice, lumber, sugar, and oil. They are required to import most of the fabricated products they use and, some of them, much of the food. Practically all the machinery and equipment needed for investment purposes must be imported. Low as their average per capita incomes are, these would fall to much lower, politically intolerable levels if world trade were seriously curtailed. It is in the field of trade that the high-income countries can take actions that will have important beneficial effects on economic development.

The efforts to reduce trade barriers through reduction or elimination of tariffs, quotas, and arbitrary financial controls can be intensified, since these barriers are a continuing handicap to economic growth at home and abroad. Adherence to the principles and policies of the General Agreement on Trade and Tariffs (GATT) can be more firmly pressed, with lesser applications of the various types of escape clauses, particularly by the more advanced countries. At the same time the highly desirable projects for the establishment of regional market areas (Western Europe, Latin America) should firmly adhere to the objective of reducing all trade barriers, rather than establishing new barriers or maintaining the existing ones. It is even more important that the major trading countries resist internal pressures to raise tariffs or, what is much worse, establish quotas, when domestic industries complain against foreign competition. To yield to this pressure would have unfavorable effects far beyond their immediate instance.

Included in the adjustment of trade policies is a reexamination of existing regulations for East-West trade. Present policies are a constant source of friction not only between East and West, but also with those countries in the Free World who feel it necessary to increase their trade. Moreover, the restrictions now are of questionable value in reducing the military build-up of the Communist bloc. Embargoes may have had the effect of reducing the rate of military build-up, but they have also stimulated the establishment of domestic sources of supply within Soviet bloc countries. Under present conditions, a reexamination of these policies could lead to increased trading opportunities for both large and small countries.

Because the underdeveloped countries are so dependent for their earnings of foreign exchange on a relatively few basic commodities, price changes in these commodities are of prime importance to them. When these prices are unusually high, they earn substantial amounts of foreign exchange and when the price drops sharply, their incomes are drastically cut. Theoretically, these countries should be able to develop the necessary governmental machinery and self-discipline required to balance the good times against the bad times, to establish reserves from the high earnings that can be used to supplement the low earnings when prices are low. In practice, this is a difficult policy even for those countries with highly advanced facilities for administration and fiscal controls; in the underdeveloped countries, it has usually proved impossible to pursue. Consequently, the additional earnings are often expended on less important imports, while during periods of low earnings, imports essential to the investment program have to be curtailed. Not only is this process wasteful of resources, but such violent fluctuations of earnings seriously handicap economic planning by both private businessmen and government agencies.

Attempts to control prices of some of these commodities under various types of stabilization schemes have usually been associated with efforts to raise these prices, or to maintain them against falling market prices. Most of these attempts have been costly failures, and the more important consumer countries, including the United States, are quite skeptical of progress along these lines. This skepticism now constitutes one of the major obstacles, not only to a solution, but even to a serious search for a solution to this important question.

Yet the problem is so important that some improvement must be made. Plans that limit the amount of price fluctuation with no attempt to raise or maintain prices over the long run may have a much better chance of success. Through the use of buffer stocks whose sales and purchases can be used to balance the market, the plan can keep prices from increasing or decreasing sharply during the marketing period, while permitting the annual average price to rise or fall gradually in response to basic demand and supply forces. Such plans may be costly to operate or self-supporting after the first investment of working capital, depending upon the shrewdness with which they are established and administered. Even the costly plans may be cheaper than the costs to both producing and consuming countries of the erratic swings of supply and demand which are now so common in international trade in basic commodities.

In most of the poorer countries, the attainment of self-sustaining economic growth will take a long time and requires long-range planning. Some of the most difficult problems faced in shifting a country from indifference and stagnation to self-generated growth are those whose solution lies in the patient acquisition of knowl-

edge, skills, attitudes, and values. Quick remedies for low agricultural productivity, low efficiency per factory worker, mass illiteracy,
the crippling need for adequate managerial skills, have not been
found and are unlikely to be discovered.

The flow of development funds and technology to the low-income countries has thus far been regarded as temporary and short-
term. Its volume has been based largely on annual decisions and
subjected to the pressures of current political situations. Mild
efforts to establish agencies on a basis longer than one year have
usually met the opposition of legislative bodies jealous of their
rights to review needs and appropriate funds annually.

The remedy is, for once, wholly in the control of the richer
countries. In recognition of this fact that the Free World has a
permanent interest in the economic growth of its poorer and richer
members alike, the annual funding of such international programs
as UN technical assistance, the UN Special Fund, and such national efforts as the International Cooperation Administration and
the Development Loan Fund should be replaced by commitments that extend from three to five years.

6

After more than a decade of experience with foreign aid, it is
clear that bilateral relationships have serious limitations, especially
when they touch on the central issues of economic and social policy, of resource allocation, and of development administration that
arise in each nation as it starts to convert economic plans into social
and administrative reality.

The crucial policy and programming decisions in economic
development raise touchy political issues, vitally affecting local
special interests, in which it is wholly inappropriate, and would
often be unwise, for another government to be directly involved.

Self-respecting sovereign nations, especially if they are new and
insecure in their sovereignty, will normally be afraid to let a power-

ful foreign government participate in the consideration of such basic questions. The United States and other high-income countries are therefore gravely handicapped—in some countries, indeed, we are effectively debarred from participation and influence in these decisions—by the bilateral groove in which most of our efforts in support of economic development have been caught.

There are two means of escape from this predicament. One is to give maximum encouragement to nongovernmental organizations such as business firms, universities, and private philanthropic foundations. Organizations such as the Ford Foundation or private technical-assistance firms like International Development Services, Inc., can often establish more intimate and effective relationships with foreign governments than a government agency could possibly do. Sometimes this principle holds even when the "private" agency is working under contract to a government agency.

The other escape, valid for the wide range of activities which can only be carried on at the government level, is to work with and through international agencies. There is a strong case for making an effective multilateral organization our primary agent for economic development and doing our best to persuade all other industrial countries to use the same agency for promoting sound progress in the emergent countries.

Such a multilateral framework would help substantially to reduce the political and psychological barriers to intimate collaboration with outsiders, to deflate the issue of "intervention," and to permit basic development problems to be considered and worked out between the emerging countries and ourselves in reasonably objective fashion. An international agency for promoting economic development, in whose establishment the countries of Asia, Africa, and Latin America have taken part, whose terms of reference they have explicitly approved, and in which they are effectively represented, cannot be regarded by them as "foreign" in the same sense as a United States Government organ (or a German or British one, or even an outside international grouping such as the European Economic Community or the one now projected for the Atlantic Community). A really multilateral agency cannot reasonably be excluded from concerning itself with its members' domestic policies and programs, for such concern is the essence of its agreed function of promoting sound development. It should be noted, however, that an international agency for promoting economic development should have the widest possible base of support; too dominant a role by one country may reproduce on an international scale the unwanted political reactions often produced by undue stress on the bilateral approach.

These may appear somewhat abstract, verbal distinctions. They have great significance in practice, however, as the experience of every international agency bears witness.

Other considerations also weigh heavily in favor of using multilateral channels in this field. High-income countries not now contributing as much resources as they should to the underdeveloped areas are placed in a position where their neglect becomes more pointed and remedial steps more advisable. A multilateral approach, moreover, provides a tangible demonstration of the participating countries' unity of interest and purpose; minimizes the danger of "development" programs being twisted into instruments of commercial rivalry among the industrial nations outside the Soviet bloc; and offers a challenging outlet for the energies of these nations, a lift for their morale potentially comparable in psychological significance to the settlement of frontier areas in the eighteenth and nineteenth centuries. For the United States, the multilateral approach also serves to discredit suspicions that persist in some circles in Europe, as well as in the underdeveloped world, that our aim is to substitute an American economic imperialism for European colonialism.

The international machinery now in existence is inadequate to the task of promoting economic development on a large scale; a larger proportion of an enlarged effort can hardly be placed under multilateral auspices until more satisfactory arrangements have been made to augment their resources and facilities. Fortunately, one can easily envisage the general form that such arrangements might take, and real progress has recently been made in the desired direction. Free World policy should give high priority to developing and trying to bring into being the most desirable organizational structure and international staff for this purpose.

The deficiencies of the international machinery now in existence are quite obvious. The UN specialized agencies are too sovereign, too much inclined toward functional particularism, and too little coordinated in rational "country programs." Their technical assistance activities, each in its special field, are largely autonomous; the Technical Assistance Board of the United Nations consists largely of the representatives of these agencies and has only tenuous coordinating authority over a part of their budgets. The technical assistance they offer and the financing provided by the World Bank (for certain types of productive investments) and the Special Fund (for preinvestment surveys or intensive studies and training) represent a "project approach" rather than a "country program approach"—that is, they are planned as specific projects with as yet too little explicit attention to the relation of these projects to one another or to a rational development program for the country concerned. Very detailed decisions on projects and budgets are made at headquarters, often through a complicated process of interagency negotiation.

Thus, the job of coordinating and integrating the work of these agencies is largely saddled onto the inexperienced, ill-staffed, overwhelmed governments of the recipient countries—which means that in many cases it is hardly done at all.

Development operations—of which investment, technical assistance, and the establishment of a policy and institutional framework are all integral parts—can be effectively coordinated only in the context of a "country program." Such a program would focus on the country's special situation and needs; concentrate especially on the strategic points in the economy where a breakthrough may be possible, that would permit rapid progress on a broader front; and take into account local resources and efforts and related assistance from all sources. Such a program would be of enormous value in enabling the contributors of external resources to weigh intelligently the country's need for (and ability to use) financial and technical assistance, to apply their contribution to the objects of highest priority, and to resist constant *ad hoc* pressures to undertake "crash" programs or dissipate their efforts in a host of marginal projects.

The ultimate responsibility for deciding what outside assistance offered shall be applied to what purposes lies, of course, with each recipient government. The United Nations has passed a number of resolutions, after extended debate in its various organs, suggesting the kinds of national programming and coordinating machinery believed to be best—recommending, for example, the establishment of interministerial committees on outside aid. But most of the less developed countries simply do not possess the technical skills or administrative machinery required both to program the implementations of a complex national development plan and to relate the efforts of from a dozen to thirty outside agencies to it. (India is a notable, but still only partial, exception.) It seems essential that some single agency take a major initiative in helping them to work it out.

The logical focus of this activity, at least as far as the international agencies are concerned, would be a strong aid director for each country with real jurisdiction over all the United Nations activities in the country to which he is accredited. Such an official should have the resources and the backing to work out a realistic national development program with the local authorities, subject to a budget for external international assistance which would be set by a central board under the general supervision of the Secretary-General of the United Nations.

Requests to the World Bank for loans or to the Special Fund for the financing of preinvestment activities should carry his recommendations, as deserving support in the context of the "country program"; otherwise they should be turned back by the financing agencies in order to emphasize the central importance of relating external aid to such a program. And a major element in any of these agencies' consideration of requests for assistance should be the country director's appraisal of the effort being made by the country itself, and the determination and intelligence with which it is facing up to the arduous tasks and painful policy decisions that sound development requires.

While the United Nations country director could not very well be given explicit authority over the bilateral programs of the United States or other high-income nations, the existence of a rational country program would put great pressure on the individual nations to relate their programs to it, just as the International Cooperation Administration and the Development Loan Fund now are seeking to relate their investment aid in India to the imperatives of the Third Five-Year Plan.

This proposal does not require a revolution in contemporary thinking about the administration of international development, but it does require a much more rapid evolution along lines which are already clearly in evidence. A forward step of major importance was taken soon after the United Nations Special Fund was established when its Managing Director decided to treat the country representatives of the Technical Assistance Board (who until then had a vague coordinating role vis-à-vis the operating personnel of the specialized agencies in the field, but virtually no resources of their own to work with) as the representatives also of the new Fund. In many countries this gives the coordinator control over more resources than the agencies he is supposed to coordinate, which is indeed an important beginning. Further steps to build up the position of the TAB representative and convert him into a UN country director on the model suggested above are urgently required. Equally urgent are steps to ensure that every such representative is the kind of experienced and knowledgeable executive who knows how to use the additional accretions of authority when he gets them.

Officials in a number of the underdeveloped countries have been quietly advocating an approach of this kind for several years, and their views have been shared by a scattering of official and unofficial voices in several of the major industrial countries. Outside the United States, much of the diffidence in broaching the subject directly seems to have stemmed from concern about United States reaction, coupled with a frank recognition that without American support no such scheme could succeed. It is worth noting that on three occasions—when the International Finance Corporation, the UN Special Fund and most recently the International Development Association were approved—once the United States Government made up its mind to endorse the concept, after years of reluctance, other major contributing countries lined up in support within a very few months, or even weeks.

7

The world-wide movement toward regional organizations has been a striking feature of international relations since World War II. It presents major opportunities for the pursuit in novel ways of the objectives of the UN charter and the policy aims of the Free World. Let us consider the main trends:

1. The weakening and then the revival of Western Europe, together with the emergence of the United States and the Soviet Union as the major rivals in a new balance of power, decreased the significance of the old European rivalries in Europe and placed a premium on putting together a Europe which would be large enough and strong enough to restore to Europeans the sense of having some influence on their own destiny.

2. Outside of Europe, the breakup of colonial empires brought into being a large number of new nations, most of them too small to be visible under modern technological conditions.

3. The United Nations seems to the leaders of most new nations to be remote from their concerns, dominated by political and security issues and by the major contestants in the Cold War. It is so huge and complicated that few countries can afford to participate seriously in its committees, boards, and working parties; partly for this reason, the UN staff is largely recruited from the more advanced countries. Nevertheless the UN is the one forum the less developed countries have for getting global consideration of economic and social issues they regard as of global import.

4. Recognizing these feelings early, the United Nations Secretariat and some of the large countries have pushed the concept of regional committees closer to home, for research and discussion about the problems of economic development. The Economic Commissions for Europe (ECE), for Asia and the Far East (ECAFE), for Latin America (ECLA), and more recently for Africa, have on the whole had good acceptance by member countries; in significant fields of common concern the members have evidently found them some use as a means of exchanging information, learning from each other, negotiating agreements on national action and of providing their own leaders with valuable experience in the conduct of international relations. Special study groups have examined problems particularly important to the different regions, with results that have contributed considerably to more consistent national policies.

By and large, these agencies have assembled competent staffs and have served well as training centers for technicians from member countries. The experience of these agencies, even within the limited purposes of research and consultation, has demonstrated in small but persuasive ways that a close and fruitful operating relationship can be developed among the countries in a region. In the Western Hemisphere, the Organization of American States has gone somewhat further than ECLA in promoting operations on a regional basis (for it has become to some extent an operating technical assistance agency) has fostered the creation of the Inter-

American Bank, and has even tested the uninviting waters of joint security arrangements.

The kinds of regional institutions that may now emerge will naturally differ from region to region.

In Western Europe, the continental grouping is a challenging political and economic creation of great importance to the Free World. Support for the new Community of Six can be provided through private investment and the expansion of trade, and through a line of political encouragement clear enough to offset efforts to create new trade barriers.

In Latin America, geographical proximity and a long history of contacts both pleasant and unpleasant have produced a special relationship with the United States, reflected in contemporary regional arrangements in which the United States is normally a full member. The question is whether the time has not come to dispel the "sphere of influence" atmosphere that still hangs over United States-Latin American relations, and to encourage both greater Latin American support of UN activities and the participation in Latin American economic development of the British and the Continental European countries, including the Community of Six.

In South and Southeast Asia the need for a more effective regional approach is underlined by the desperate urge (and need) for economic development, the strong aversion to participation in the Cold War, the growing importance of China as an example of rapid growth and as a military aggressor and a major economic factor in the region, and the possibility that India and Japan can together organize a serious counterweight to the growing influence of Communist China. Since both present and probably future political leaders of all the countries in the region are irrevocably if not always effectively committed to economic development and in varying degrees are allergic to political and military alignment, the best approach to regional institution building would seem to be some form of regional development organization as the primary channel of investment capital into the area. Such an agency could be staffed and operated primarily by Asians, with limited participation by non-Asian technical advisors.

In the Middle East the knottiest problem appears to be the development of responsible Arab leadership. One way to help on this score is to assist the Arab States to set in motion the Arab Financial Institution, which is already in an advanced stage of planning. The violent "nationalistic" feelings of most of the Arab leaders, as well as logic, preclude the growth of any development institution other than one controlled and operated by the people of the region. There is in fact a regional kind of nationalism, a tenuous unity in the Arab world that may in time transcend the many elements of distrust and the arbitrary national borders of the States carved up so casually after World War I. If this drive can be channeled into constructive regional development, it may help produce the type of leadership capable in time of dealing with—indeed, welcoming, in view of manpower needs—the presence of a million refugees; recognizing the *fait accompli* of the State of Israel, and exploiting the opportunities for converting Middle East oil into regional production capacity, instead of siphoning these resources off into investment portfolios in London and conspicuous consumption by princes in the Arabian peninsula.

In Africa south of the Sahara, two levels of regionalism are in prospect. The small nations emerging from British and French rule, such as Ghana, Nigeria, and Guinea in West Africa, and Tanganyika and Kenya in East Africa, must surely look forward to federal combinations in order to develop units large enough to survive as independent nations in the modern world. The process will be painful, perhaps chaotic. It will be enormously complicated by the lack of accepted or acceptable leaders and, in the "white settler" countries, the growing racial bitterness there.

Beyond the African federations there may be room for a regional approach to some of the problems common to all the emerging ex-colonies. One of these is the universal lack of trained administrators. In Africa the gap between what the new governments can do and what they are expected to do is so wide that technical and administrative help often cannot merely take the form of "advice." In many cases foreign experts will find themselves working inside African governments; such a pattern is already established on a large scale in Ethiopia, and in small, tentative ways in Ghana and Nigeria. OPEX, the new United Nations program to provide international administrators for operating jobs within the less developed countries, may in time prove to be of major significance in Africa.

Briefly, then, the political leaders of smaller countries, by setting up regional organizations that are directly responsive to the constituent members, can feel that their futures are largely, if not entirely, under their control. It is in their interest and ours that they should come to have this feeling.

8

There is a continuing, growing need to dissociate foreign economic assistance from both the appearance and reality of support of existing regimes and of resistance to change. Change is the essence of the modernizing process: changes in institutions and cultures, changes in technology and the way capital is formed, changes in government and social relations. To have programs that support economic development branded as resisting change is both disabling and ironic, for these same programs are among the most effective stimulants of change. Yet a survey would show that, because governments in many poor countries come from the wealthier or landowning classes or other elements reluctant to encourage necessary social change, foreign aid programs have been widely though generally falsely identified as opposing "progress."

Few countries are so stable in their institutions and patterns of political behavior that the continuation of the present governmental setup, with its class structure, its ambitions and dominant interests, can be confidently expected to remain constant over any considerable period of time. The close identification of foreign assistance with a particular government in power clearly creates operational and policy problems when that government is changing or when it is resisting pressures for social and political changes.

Yet while change is inevitable, not all changes are desirable. A successful foreign assistance program, whether it is channeled through bilateral or multilateral agencies, can influence and reinforce the changes that serve the basic wants of modern man while attempting to slow down or modify those changes that do not. Therefore, resistance to the wrong kind of change has its place in an aid program, but cannot be the prime objective of foreign economic assistance to the less developed countries.

The operating policy that supports programs rather than regimes and selects the kinds of programs that induce change—land reform, education, health, transportation and communication, many industrialization projects, and the development of natural resources —avoids the serious consequences of appearing to resist desired change. Support of specific programs can be direct, even when authorized through government channels, and public understanding of this relationship is not too difficult to achieve. Under these conditions, most changes in government need not materially affect this direct relationship.

The key to effective operations in the economic and social sphere is not to mistake the technical purpose (changing the tenure system, preventing disease, building schools or railways or factories) for the more fundamental purpose of building an institutional fabric that will contain and rationalize the "modernization" effort, enable the government to spur the development process at all levels (not merely to set theoretical goals in a national plan), and provide a channel for wide participation in development administration by the people who are affected by it.

To sponsor activities which *per se* commend themselves to

large groups of people and therefore promise to commend themselves to the "next government"; to build institutions and programs rather than mere formal intergovernmental relationships—
these policies do *not* require the snubbing or bypassing of existing
governments. Quite the contrary: all foreign programs operate
with the approval and support of existing governments. The latter
request and approve projects, regulate the flow of foreigners in
and out of the country, and accept many of the related financial
and administrative burdens.

What a policy of supporting programs rather than supporting
regimes *can* do is:

1. avoid "shadow projects" that advertise improvements but are
designed primarily to benefit groups in power;

2. emphasize a few long-term programs of major significance,
rather than a host of miscellaneous small projects which may
fit some theory of "program balance" but make it hard for people
at large to form any clear image of the purposes of foreign participation in economic development; and

3. enhance the value of working through multilateral organization programs, which when astutely managed can become deeply
involved in the touchiest "domestic" decisions of member countries without raising issues of national sovereignty.

9

During the last decade, the Gross National Product of the
United States economy has grown about 3.5 per cent a year, in
real terms. Western European rates of growth during the same
period were higher, averaging (also in real terms) about 6 per
cent a year. Similarly, the over-all annual increase in Latin America during the past decade has been quite vigorous—4.5 per
cent a year—although the variation among countries is very great.
In Asia and Africa, exclusive of Communist China, the annual
rates were much lower, probably averaging about 2.5 to 3 per cent

a year. There the increase in production of goods and services is barely ahead of the increase in population, which is between 1.5 and 2 per cent a year.

The absence of reliable production statistics makes these estimates of rates of growth difficult to evaluate. Yet it appears reasonable to assert that over the past decade the quantity of goods and services available to the mass of people in the underdeveloped areas has increased only slightly—far less, in both absolute and relative terms, than in the advanced countries of the Free World. In other words, the poor countries have become relatively poorer.

Economists and other social scientists may not have yet developed a wholly satisfactory general theory of economic growth, but their analyses have succeeded in demonstrating, with a high degree of assurance, that certain factors are necessary, if not sufficient, in the process of growth; among these, the appropriate role of government is important and may even be decisive. In economically advanced countries, growth requires appropriate monetary and fiscal policies, together with positive actions to encourage international trade and to strengthen the machinery for international payments. In underdeveloped countries, economic growth requires, in addition to the above, the inflow of substantial amounts of capital, together with the technical assistance required to attract and utilize this capital in the transformation of a traditional society into a modern one.

Estimates of the amount of additional funds now needed for the world's less developed areas depend not only on the rate of growth assumed as the objective but also, and perhaps primarily, on the ability of the countries to utilize foreign capital efficiently. Judgments about the projected levels of efficiency vary with almost every observer in the field. Each expert projection makes different assumptions as to the desired pattern of development, the efficiency of capital use, the ability of the country to raise and use domestic capital, the rate of private foreign investment, the capacity of the nation's leaders to build the necessary political and social institutions, and a host of other equally important factors that are quite impossible to project with accuracy.

An arresting and authoritative estimate of resource requirements was made early in 1960 by Paul G. Hoffman, Managing Director of the United Nations Special Fund. Most previous studies, he points out, "converge in the neighborhood of $3 billion per year" of additional funds required to provide for an extra one per cent per annum of per capital growth in the underdeveloped countries.

His proposal is precisely stated:

That we—all of us together—fix it as our goal to double in the 1960's as compared with the 1950's, the annual per capita rate of economic growth in 100 countries and territories containing a billion and a quarter of the world's people. If we achieve this goal it will mean increasing the per capita economic growth rate of the less developed countries from an average of 1 per cent a year in the 1950's to an average of 2 per cent in the 1960's. To do this it will be necessary for the less developed countries to sustain an annual rate of economic growth of 4 per cent. This will mean a total increase of about 40 per cent and a per capita increase of nearly 25 per cent in 10 years. It will mean increasing per capita income from the estimated present figure of around $100 to around $125 in 1970. This means increasing per capita income in the 1960's by about 25 per cent per person or an average of about $2.50 per person per year.

To achieve this rate of economic growth, Mr. Hoffman reaches the following conclusions about the needs for foreign capital:

All in all, it seems reasonable to proceed on the assumption that something in the neighborhood of $3 billion a year—$30 billion over the decade from outside sources—will be required to maintain an extra 1 per cent per annum of growth per person as compared with the 1950's.

In my view it seems likely that as much as $10 billion of this required $30 billion will be covered in the 1960's through increases (over present levels) in private investment, and through increases in existing bilateral and multilateral aid and investment programs (e.g., the Development Loan Fund). This leaves something on the order of $20 billion which has to be found, during the 1960's, from sources which are at present not available. This $20 billion is the missing link in the chain upon which satisfatory progress in the economic development of the world during the next decade depends. This figure is not a firm one, for it is impossible to make a hard and fast prediction. Some suggest that the deficiency may be as little as $15 billion; others put it at $30 billion. My guess of $2 billion a year presupposes a continuing expansion of world trade and an heroic effort on the part of the underdeveloped countries to increase their own exports and savings. Neither seems an unreasonable assumption. It should be emphasized that additional capital supplied from the outside, including the proposed increase, would be only the smaller part of the total investment that would occur in the less developed countries. The larger part would of course come out of their own savings and the success of the development program would depend in considerable measure upon the extent to which the governments of the less developed countries will be able to increase local savings and channel them into investment in productive enterprise.

This emphasis on the need for additional capital does not imply an assumption that capital deficiency is the only or even the major obstacle to be overcome. Clearly, more capital is needed if the rate of annual per capital economic growth is to be doubled over the decade ahead of us. It is equally clear that many changes in social institutions and values, with their attendant increases in knowledge and communication, are also essential to the processes of economic development. Who is to say which element is most important, when the absence or scarcity of any one of them so seriously limits the rate and character of economic growth?

Even more characteristic of underdeveloped countries than capital deficiency is the absence of many major prerequisites to the effective use of capital, such as inadequate knowledge about their natural resources and a lack of sufficient trained manpower to modernize their countries. These inadequacies seriously lower the effectiveness of past investment and reduce the incentives for additional investment.

Consequently, programs for the training of manpower in under-developed countries must be given a higher priority than at present. A society that is modernizing itself requires a large number of skilled workers, artisans, managers, technicians, and professional personnel, coming from a largely literate population capable of communicating within the complicated framework of a modern society. Without such strategic skilled manpower and improved communications, modernization on a broad scale becomes almost impossible.

To develop this type of manpower from a tradition-bound and predominantly illiterate society is not impossible, but it is assuredly both expensive and time-consuming. While it may be possible to develop specific types of skilled construction workers and machine operators fairly rapidly from unskilled peasants, more time is needed to train (through practical experience) the managers, technicians, and professional personnel. Although some countries have bettered this mark in the postwar period, in most cases it will take ten to fifteen years to develop the managers, engineers, and technicians required to operate effectively such complex organizations as steel mills, power stations, and textile factories. Some of the requirements for trained personnel can be met ad interim by using foreigners, but the largest part of the need for trained personnel can be met only by the less developed countries themselves.

The importance of developing managers and technicians does not, however, imply that specialized advanced training should be accorded an overriding priority in development planning.

A generally literate population is so basic to a modern society that the rapid achievement of general literacy also deserves the highest possible priority. Like so many other problems confronting the poor countries, there can be no "lesser evil" in the choice between specialized and general educational programs.

Another vital preinvestment need is for surveys of natural resources, and the creation of industrial research institutes, and the study of the relative development potential of each emergent country. Without this type of information, investment will be either delayed or inefficient, or both. Preinvestment functions are now stimulated by a large number of bilateral programs and international agencies as well as some private endeavors.

The newest international agency in this field, the United Nations Special Fund, has been specifically established to aid the development of low-income countries precisely by financing preinvestment activities such as resource surveys, technical training, and field research.

But the United Nations Special Fund was organized many years after it was needed and then financed with inadequate funds. The annual goal of $100 million, modest as that is compared with requirements for preinvestment operations, has been only partially met; in 1959, $26 million was actually made available and its resources for 1960 are about $38 million. In the whole range of national and international activity designed to spur economic development, support for this effort to break preinvestment bottlenecks has a very special importance.

If the high-income countries should undertake a major increase in the provision of capital to the less developed areas, an important part of these added resources will in one way or another be collected by the government from the people at large. Increased taxes are always unpleasant to contemplate, and there is usually no way of avoiding the fact that to assemble the resources for overseas transfer by government will require increased taxes in some form. But the form is important, and in this field one of the best and most available forms of some of the required transfer is that of surplus agricultural commodities.

Agricultural surpluses may have become a more or less permanent problem for the United States economy and certain other countries. A basic reason for the surplus is the presence of powerful economic incentives to high production, including an ingenious variety of government subsidies and guarantees. But another cause is the astonishing increase in productivity on the farm; in the United States this has meant a greater increase in productivity since 1940 than in the previous one hundred and twenty years. There seems no good reason to suppose that the rate of increase in productivity will decline during the next decade.

At the present rate of use, the sale of surpluses for local currency under Public Law 480 and their procurement under the Mutual Security Act are not sufficient to reduce the large stores of commodities already available. The modifications of the farm price-support program that have thus far been proposed do not appear to be sufficiently broad to "solve" this problem at its source. Nor is any other mild tinkering with present schemes likely to produce more effective results. Eventually, the rising population in the United States and the world may cause agricultural surpluses to disappear, but this is at most a long-term factor, something for the 1970's rather than the 1960's; moreover, it is offset in part by continuing increases in productivity and the opening of new lands for irrigation and production.

A partial answer, one that should be more thoroughly explored, might be the substitution of massive "production contracts" for the existing methods of sale of surplus commodities. Under such a plan, the United States could enter into credit agreements, stretching over five to ten years, to provide large quantities of specific agricultural commodities, priced at world market prices. Although they would be financed by government funds, the commodities could move in regular commercial channels and not necessarily as government-to-government shipments.

To the recipients of these surplus commodities, a credit for the supply of surplus commodities over a long period of time would permit some of the less developed countries to devote their limited resources to the more productive projects, rather than emphasizing food production almost regardless of cost. In other words, very large amounts of additional surplus agricultural commodities can, if properly planned, represent increased real resources for capital formation, rather than just increased consumption, necessary and desirable as that may be.

For other countries exporting these same agricultural commodities, the long-term credits for the purchases of United States commodities may resemble export dumping less than present methods of surplus disposal. Some of these countries might even be induced to join a series of credits, as part of joint efforts to make more resources available to the underdeveloped countries of the Free World.

10

It would not be difficult to prolong for many pages this discussion of what the high-income countries can do to stimulate economic growth in the low-income countries. While the activities mentioned seem the most important ones, they by no means exhaust the list of possible initiatives. Greater encouragement to private foreign investment, establishment of payments unions, expanded research in production and distribution, improvement in specialized fields of administration—the list can grow much longer, for the process of economic growth is as complex and comprehensive as modern society itself.

We have stressed the obligations of the high-income countries; the opportunities have been taken perhaps too much for granted. A wider fulfillment of man's basic wants both assumes and assures economic growth and a morale-building sense of purpose in the advanced countries. So curious is the process of economic growth that by giving more, the high-income countries will receive more. In our interdependent world, the involvement in one another's affairs is mutual—but the benefits that result are mutual, too.

The quality of political judgment displayed by the electorates of the three main Western democracies, the United States, Britain, France, is of vital importance. For the power of electorates to dismiss one government and set up another obviously determines the course of policy. No statesman, no diplomat, no politician can carry through a policy which runs counter to the mood of the voters, to what the politician is apt to call "the climate of opinion." That is the basic factor in the situation now confronting us.

Only improvement in that climate, better mass understanding, will enable the Western democracies to achieve by the method of freedom a unity comparable to the greater unity of the Communist world; a Western unity which is indispensable if Communist pressures are to be resisted, the more liberal and humane elements of a free society preserved; and peace maintained.

—SIR NORMAN ANGELL

4

ENDS AND MEANS OF
COMMUNICATION

Harry S. Ashmore

Not long ago *The New York Times* ran a news report from Washington under this headline:

U.S. SHUNS TALKS

IN SOVIET ON POLIO

The dispatch told the mournful story of a decision by the State Department forbidding attendance by three physicians employed by the United States Government at a Moscow meeting of scientists called to receive reports on the first large-scale testing of live virus antipolio vaccine—a vaccine, incidentally, developed in this country but never put to extensive use here.

The State Department's decision was taken over the protest of the United States Public Health Service. The stated reason was that polio experts from Communist China and East Germany were to be present at the Moscow conference, and it was feared that contact between American officials and representatives of these regimes might imply "recognition" or give them "prestige." The Department did grant visas to three private physicians.

Here, clearly, was a failure of communications of a peculiarly painful sort—one that hampers a humane undertaking, and one that conceivably could deprive our own public health service of information upon which the lives of American children might depend.

The immediate instrument of this failure is a single government. But the underlying cause is an international political condition for which no nation can escape some degree of blame. All around the globe doors to the free movement of people, of information and ideas have been slammed shut—and they have been pried open again, if at all, only by an arduous process of official bargaining and negotiation.

Important gains have been made. Even while the State Department was denying the three doctors the right to attend the Moscow conference, six American scientists were preparing to depart for Moscow for a bilateral conference with their Soviet opposite numbers. The number of these contacts is still small, but it is growing—and a few years ago there were none at all in important areas of the world.

The deep-seated political divisions among nations, the ideological, religious, and cultural differences among peoples, and the resulting international tensions may in time be eased by technological progress and change, but so far the evidence indicates that the process has accentuated them. Rapidly improving means of communication have shrunk our world, and will continue to do so, but the mere drawing together of people cannot in itself reduce tensions. On the contrary, new proximity may make hitherto remote possibilities of conflict of interest seem, and perhaps be, imminent; the reduction of the ocean barriers by the airplane and the rocket has created new demands for national security— and these demands, more often than not, have been met by restrictions on the free passage of persons and of ideas.

We can see the effects of this condition at home and abroad.

The tradition of the United States is that of the open society— of free speech, free movement, self-determination of peoples, of trade as free as the frequently disputed realities of the international market place will permit. We assume these freedoms for our own citizens; our professed foreign policy is to encourage their attainment by all peoples everywhere. Yet, under the pressures of the Cold War we have seen these freedoms reduced in our own country by government policy. In the name of military security substantial areas of publicly financed activity are no longer available to the public view. Official restrictions have been placed on the entry of foreigners and even on the movement of our own nationals. The government has come to rely heavily upon the official dissemination of information, and inevitably to assume a role of advocacy for the official point of view, both at home and abroad.

Under our system this process has required the consent of the people, and has received it. But that consent has resulted in part from the interaction of our free institutions as private citizens assume personal responsibility in the name of national security. An American who hates and fears a foreign ideology is free to condemn and oppose it as an individual, or as a member of voluntary associations that share his view—and there is no effective official test of truth or wisdom that may be applied to his actions and utterances. Thus he may play a positive role in shaping public policy or the performance of the private media of communications.

In other nations the means are different but the effect is often the same. In an authoritarian state the ruling power may by fiat impose restraints against the dissident idea whatever its source, and here tradition supports the action. Entry of travelers and publications from abroad may be limited or barred, and radio beams jammed; nationals may be confined within their borders as a safeguard against corrupting influences. Official propagandists may use their control of radio, television, and the press deliberately to distort the image of the outside world to serve the ends of the governing body.

Under the Western tradition the total control and calculated employment of the means of communication as an instrument of state policy is an intolerable threat to freedom.

Under the authoritarian tradition—and the apparent necessity of survival for governments newly come to independence by armed or peaceful revolution—the toleration of error and of dissent inherent in a free system of communications is unthinkable.

Philosophically, the twain are not likely to meet any time soon. Any program for improving communications must take into account this reality. It must also concede the possibility that the removal of barriers to communications may not reduce world tensions, in the short haul at least, but may increase them by permitting sustained conflict between the two competing systems at many sensitive points.

2

Louis Lyons of the Nieman Foundation has set forth a handy classification of the two primary kinds of barriers to effective international communication:

• Official barriers maintained by governments, through censorship, secrecy, exclusions, and restrictions or handicaps imposed on correspondents, travelers, publications, broadcasts, and mail.

• Private barriers created by insufficient resources, enterprise, or interest on the part of the communications media, educational and other organizations, and individuals.

The distinction is an important one in the consideration of any program of action. The first area is clearly within the province of government; the role of private organizations is limited to the encouragement and promotion of official action. In Western terms the situation is reversed in the second area; here operative action must come from private individuals and organizations, with government cast in the role of providing encouragement and perhaps financial support. While this distinction cannot be applied with precision to authoritarian nations, where all concerned institutions are under public operation, it would appear that it can be applied to a significant degree; if in Russia, for example, we can assume a continued relaxation of the once-rigid policy of excluding all Western ideas and culture, we can also assume pressure from organizations of scientists, artists, businessmen, farmers, and the like for formal and informal contact with their foreign contemporaries.

In any event, it will be seen that when the first set of official barriers is totally in effect the second is meaningless. This is presently the case with two of the great powers, the United States and Communist China. Significantly, however, there are considerable pressures on both governments for resolution or at least reduction of the impasse; they come externally from other concerned powers, but they also come from within. In China these are doubtless primarily official considerations of economic and political advantage to be gained through the achievement of diplomatic relations with the United States. In the United States the pressures come from a variety of sources, and have been countered by sources dedicated to support of Nationalist China. Aside from its public concern over the complex issue of recognition for Communist China, the American communications industry also has exerted its influence in the practical matter of gaining access to the Chinese mainland for its correspondents. Opinion within the industry is divided over whether the media have done all they could in altering the restrictive policies of the State Department. But certainly much has been done, and there have been more or less continuous negotiations over a period of years, with representatives of the American Society of Newspaper Editors taking the lead.

This sort of bargaining between a private, unofficial agency and the government of the United States is a symbol of the new complications in international relations. It is inherently repugnant to the American tradition for newspaper correspondents or other private citizens to become the subject of negotiation, even barter, between governments; the assumption of a more innocent age was that Americans should have the right to go where they wanted and write what they liked about what they saw, and that the same privileges should be extended to foreigners who wanted to come to America—at least in the absence of a shooting war. If this was never entirely the practice, it at least provided the basis for a working theory of journalistic relations, which is no longer effective in vast areas of the world.

The official barriers to communication between the United States and Red China are not different in kind from those that exist in other important areas. Where they have been effectively lowered between Eastern and Western nations in the course of the recent thawing of the Cold War, this has been the result, initially at least, of international negotiation at the very highest level. The exchange of persons, and of information, has proceeded under rigid formulae and has not approximated anything that could be called genuinely free movement. Even so, the record is generally encouraging; so far there has been a steady increase in the kind of interchanges permitted, which must indicate that both parties regard the experiment to date as generally successful and mutually useful.

It is ironic that one of the first major breakthroughs has come in the very area which originally produced the most urgent demands for security restrictions—in the exchange of scientists and scientific information.

While ideological differences still color the relations between Eastern and Western scientists, the scientists themselves contend that in practice they are usually able to set them aside in the service of "one master—scientific truth." The scientists thus feel they may be setting the pattern for similar cooperation at all levels. Something like this was certainly the case in the recent Geophysical Year when teams of scientists from all the major nations cooperated amicably and fruitfully under arrangements that involved many nonscientists—including the military.

Pure scientists may agree on the pursuit of a common truth, but the same condition does not necessarily apply in the political order.

Indeed, the experience in the expanding contacts between Russians and Americans at this level has emphasized the practical impossibility of a Western philosopher's proceeding from a given set of premises to the conclusion reached through the exercise of Marxist dialectics. In this area there is honest disagreement over what is truth and what is error—and from this condition, as well as from the calculated efforts of conspirators and propagandists, flow some of the gross distortions in popular images.

William Benton, publisher of the *Encyclopaedia Britannica*, has written, in the *Yale Review*, of his experience in a series of interviews with the editors of the *Great Soviet Encyclopedia*. The Russian editor-in-chief told him: "Our editors' main task is to create a universal reference work. We strive to maintain complete objectivity. But all articles are of course written from the position of our world outlook—Marxism-Leninism." The extent to which this determines the result was exemplified by Benton's request that the editors select an article that might be used in both the *Britannica* and the Soviet encyclopedia. They agreed, after some hesitation, that if one could be found it probably would deal with some purely scientific matter such as cosmogony or theoretical physics.

After reading in translation the 85,000-word article on the United States in the current *Great Soviet Encyclopedia*, Benton wrote:

[It] can only be called a fantastic combination of information, ignorance, and distortion. Yet I feel it would be a mistake for us to assume that it was written tongue-in-cheek, merely in line with the fiat of the Council of Ministers; or even to assume that such of its errors as seem to spring from Marxist-Leninist doctrine are inevitable, given the Soviet system. Some part of the distortion has been due to the sequestration of Soviet scholars from the stream of non-Communist thought.

The reverse of this has been seen in our own country. As much from habits of thought and absence of information as from the baleful effect of conscious propaganda, most of us have acquired a vastly distorted view of the Soviet Union. When the barriers were finally lowered and Americans could again travel with some free-dom within the country, many were astounded at the material progress they found there, and frankly said so. And it is fair to say that the country as a whole sustained a severe psychological shock when the first Russian satellite appeared in the sky; we had come to believe that the Soviets were far behind us in technology, and we had not yet accustomed ourselves to the demonstrable fact that in many important areas they were well ahead.

3

This recitation of the sometimes polar differences in the organi-zation and the philosophy of the two dominant governmental systems that now divide the world also points to the urgent need for finding realistic accommodations in the area of international communications.

Recognizing the risks and the difficulties, I would myself argue that the United States should reaffirm its faith in the open society and base its relevant diplomacy upon this historic concept. This does not mean an automatic end to the complex multilateral nego-tiations that deal with communications as an aspect of larger policy questions; it does suggest that all possibilities of unilateral action on the part of the United States should be explored. It calls for a posture of boldness, for a willingness to lower some of the barriers of our own erection antecedent to a demand that others follow suit. It means action on our own motion wherever prac-ticable, rather than a reflex toward greater restrictions made in response to conditions dictated by others.

Accepting this thesis, however, would still leave a series of pertinent questions:

1. It is practical for the United States to permit temporary visits by foreign nationals, without regard to their ideology or political affiliation?

2. Should the United States place no arbitrary limit on the num-

ber of visitors who would be accepted in any category, except the practical ones having to do with self-support and available accommodations for journalists, scholars, scientists, and other special categories?

3. Is it practical for the United States to take affirmative action in either of the two areas cited above in the case of Communist China, without resuming diplomatic relations? Are there other nations which should be specifically exempted from such general provisions?

4. Should the United States consider offering to abandon such parts of its overseas information program as might fall within the accepted definition of propaganda in return for agreement by other nations to do the same? Is it possible to define and clearly limit the legitimate function of any government in informing other peoples about its activities and its nation's culture? If it were, would it by practically possible to apply such tests to communications agencies which function wholly under government operation and control?

5. Can the United States rely upon private communications agencies, educational and cultural institutions, and individuals traveling for private purposes to present its proper image where an open society does not exist, or where an open society cannot be brought into being? Or must the government continue to maintain and perhaps expand its official agencies of information?

The first four of these questions deal directly with action by government. They assume that the steps envisioned would be taken in the expectation that they would lead to similar action by other nations, or at least would provide additional moral leverage to bring about that end. The fifth question carries over into the area of nonofficial barriers. In that regard these questions seem relevant:

6. Does the United States government presently lend adequate financial and diplomatic support to those programs of exchange of persons and information now operated by private educational,

scientific, and cultural and religious institutions? Can the government be expected to lend substantial financial support to these undertakings without at the same time exerting direct policy control over them?

7. Is the government doing all it can to further the commercial circulation of American newspapers, magazines, books, films, radio and television broadcasts, and performing artists? Are the present limited subsidy arrangements justifiable? If so, are they adequate?

8. Is there a need for more accurate and complete information on foreign affairs for domestic consumption in the United States? If so, what can government and/or private organizations and institutions do to encourage greater concentration in these areas by the commercial communications media?

Proper answers to these questions would not alone spell out any sweeping change in American policy as it relates to international communications—nor is it suggested that all relevant possibilites have been raised. But if we start by asking the right questions, a significant alteration in the tone of American policy might be achieved, and with it new hope for greater and more productive traffic among the peoples of the world.

THE TENSIONS OF INEQUALITY
—*Two Cases*

A. The Emergence of West Africa

W. Arthur Lewis

Sixty-five million people, in sixteen different countries, live in West Africa, the vast area lying below the Sahara Desert, and stretching from the Atlantic Ocean in the West to the Cameroons in the East. Half this population lives in one country, the former British colony of Nigeria, which has 32 million people. Next in size is Ghana, with only 5 million. Only three others have more than 3 million people. So with the exception of Nigeria, we are dealing with a large number of small countries whose typical population is only about 2 millions, spread rather thinly over the ground. And all these countries are now self-governing, or soon will be.

Among the many problems of the area, let us focus on five sources of tension:

• The division of the area into British and French spheres of influence.

• The lack of education, which helps to maintain that division.

• The mix-up of tribes and religions, which menaces the stability of each of these states.

• Frontier questions.

• The federal idea, which is meant to reduce tensions, but which actually increases them.

2

Take first the division of the area among the metropolitan powers. In 1957 there was one independent state, Liberia, which was really a satellite of the United States of America. Apart from this there were four British colonies, ten French colonies, and one substantial Portuguese colony. These divisions still have important cultural, economic, and political consequences.

Culturally, there is virtually no exchange between French and British. French Africans and British Africans have no means of communication with each other. The British African intellectuals know what is happening in London, whether in the markets, or in the theater, or in politics. The French Africans know what is happening in Paris, whether in philosophy or at the opera. But neither knows anything about what is happening in the other African countries.

There is similar economic isolation. Currencies are exchanged only with difficulty. Transport facilities, whether roads, railways, or harbors, have been designed for political and not for economic convenience. Trade is parceled up by tariffs. Above all, there is political isolation, which is a continuing obstacle to the removal of other barriers. The French territories, although claiming independence, remain deeply attached to France, by sentimental as well as by economic ties, and are a little frightened of Ghana and Nigeria. French Africans and British Africans do not feel at home with each other, and it is going to take a lot of working together as independent states before they agree to break down some of the barriers that now separate them.

The second weakness of these countries is their lack of education. When Ghana became independent only one per cent of her children were receiving a high school education, and that is typical of the whole area. Thus, though these countries become independent, they continue to depend upon the outside world to run their affairs. In the government, the Ministers are African, but the civil servants and technicians are still British or French. So also the whole of large-scale private business is run by foreigners. Thus the dependence on Britain or on France is maintained. A second consequence is that the cost of any kind of development is very high, since it has to be done with foreign staff paid at higher rates than they earn in their own countries; this, for example, is a formidable obstacle to industrialization on a competitive basis.

Another consequence of the educational shortage is that some desirable developments cannot be undertaken. Every society is kept going by the products of the high school, who become teachers, nurses, secretaries, or junior administrators or technicians. Most of the obvious types of development are hindered by a shortage of people at these levels. Nothing could do more to put West Africa on its feet than a large program of high school education.

The third source of tension on which we are focusing is the fact that none of these countries is homogeneous. Each is a mixture of tribes, languages, and religions, without any sense of common history or of common nationhood. This is poor material for democracy. Many adjacent tribes are traditional enemies, having fought each other regularly right up to the beginning of the twentieth century.

The new rulers in West Africa are trying to create modern states where national loyalties are to take the place of tribal loyalties. At the same time they are for the most part revolutionaries, in the sense that they wish to break the power of tribal chiefs, and to advance the status of the common man as against the old family oligarchies. In these circumstances, politics is inevitably rough; its weapons are not so much the newspaper and the microphone as the knife, the club, and the prison cell. At my last count, in five of these countries the Opposition had no seats in Parliament, and in three other Parliaments the government had more than 80 per

cent of the seats. This has external, as well as internal consequences, for the attitude of the dictator of one country toward the
dictator of another country is more often enmity than fellow
feeling. Each country praises its own democracy, while looking with
scorn and fear at the other's dictatorship.

This hostility is at its greatest where frontiers are disputed—our
fourth source of tension. This is the case in three areas, involving
Ghana, the Cameroons, and Gambia. The metropolitan powers
kept only small forces in West Africa—even now Ghana's army
has only six thousand men. Unfortunately there are signs that this
happy state may not long persist. In view of current threats, this is
just the right time to promote in West Africa a convention for the
limitations of armaments.

The fifth source of tension, which might be a solution for all
the others, is the idea of a federation of West African states. Three
federal solutions have competed in West Africa. First there was the
possibility that the French territories would form one federation
and the British territories another. This was decisively rejected. As
soon as Ghana became independent it proceeded to destroy all its
links with the other British territories—the common airline, the
common currency, and the common research services—claiming
that it could not continue in partnership with other territories
which were still in colonial status.

In the same way, as soon as the French territories received self-
government, they destroyed the existing federation of French West
Africa. In place of this latter was offered the possibility of federation with France, in the French Community. This was at first
accepted by all the French territories except Guinea, which became
independent. Now others are following Guinea's example.

Finally there is the idea, championed by Ghana and by Guinea,
of a federation of all West African states. In present circumstances
this can hardly come to pass. The leaders distrust each other too
much, and are not being subjected to the kind of outside pressures which seem to be a necessary prerequisite for federation.

Nevertheless, this is the topic of the day. Ghana and Guinea have already announced a union, and though this has not come to much, they are busily engaged in summoning conferences of other African leaders to work out a wider West African union. They can expect no help from Britain or from France whose commonwealth aspirations are at first sight incompatible with local unions. However, the more serious danger is that aggressive initiatives by Ghana and by Guinea may frighten rather than conciliate other West African countries.

3

So much for this brief account of the five sources of tension. Because it focuses exclusively on tensions, it risks creating a false picture of West Africa as a country grimy with hatreds and oppressions. This is not how most West Africans feel. Politics touches the lives of very few. In West Africa, as in so many other parts of the world, the rule of life, for the great majority of the people, is to find out who is in power and vote for him. While life in the capital cities is politically exciting, and the newspapers resound with speeches and threats, the excitements of life in the country, for the great mass of the people, are in economic progress—in new roads, new water supplies, new schools, buses, electricity, hospitals, and other such fruits of progress, which are expanding rapidly throughout this area. West Africa is really a quiet and prosperous place, except for handfuls of political leaders who are jockeying for position with each other. This jockeying has dangerous potentialities, because it may inflame the area, but at present its dangers are confined to the relatively few who choose to play this game.

Until independence came, the outside world was represented by Britain and by France, who were anxious to maintain their monopoly. When it was proposed shortly after the war that the United Nations should enter the area, either through a Regional

Commission or through establishing regional headquarters of the Specialized Agencies, Britain and France refused and hastily created, along with other colonial powers, a new body called the Committee for Technical Cooperation in Africa South of the Sahara to keep the United Nations, the United States, and all other intruders out of Africa. However, the withdrawal of Britain and France from parts of West Africa has at once been followed by the entry of the United States, of the United Nations, and of the USSR.

Russia is well established in Guinea, and is building up an Embassy in Ghana. West African politicians have a divided mind on this subject. Some, as in Nigeria or the Ivory Coast, argue that if you play with fire you will get burned, and they will therefore not establish relations with Russia. Others, as in Guinea and in Ghana, believe that the dignity of Africans requires them to have the same freedom to have Embassies from Communist nations as is enjoyed by London or Paris or Washington. Besides, a Russian Embassy has its uses in the quest for economic aid. Ghanaian politicians say to London and to Washington "If you do not lend us £150,000,000 to build our new aluminum works, we will get the money from Moscow." Since there is no evidence that Moscow is willing to hand over £150,000,000, the British merely smile at this, but Americans are probably more nervous. What is certain is that no African politician wants his country to become a Russian satellite.

4

The outside world can help West Africa by giving aid, by helping to create an international framework, and by maintaining friendly criticism.

Technical aid is very necessary in view of the lack of education. West Africa needs hundreds of administrators and scientists, and has specially welcomed the beginnings of the United Nations

Civil Service—the OPEX. Thousands of teachers are needed, and of course a considerable inflow of capital, both private and public. West Africans would welcome an enlargement of United Nations aid in all these fields, but they will take aid from whatever source it comes, provided that it does not menace their independence. Current flows are small, a mere fraction of what is needed.

Since West Africans find it hard to come together to solve their own problems because of mutual jealousies, the outside world can help in a relevant way by extending the services of international organizations on a regional basis.

The United Nations Economic Commission for Africa, and the regional conferences of such bodies as the Food and Agriculture Organization and the International Labor Organization provide a framework for bringing West Africans together against a wider world background. Private international organizations and private foundations are also effective in bringing West Africans together in circumstances where purely African initiatives might be less effective. It is still possible that the West Africans may create enough of a federal system of their own to grapple with such obstacles as tariffs, currencies, passports, transmissible diseases, the nationalistic organization of scientific research, and the peculiar design of transportation systems. All these are matters, however, which can be hammered at within the framework of existing international institutions.

Indeed the United Nations has also the opportunity to show what it can do in solving frontier problems and in preventing war. If the Cold War can be kept out of West Africa, the Security Council may find itself quite usefully occupied in sorting out West African political disputes over the next ten years or so, such as the disputes between Ghana and her neighbors, or between Gambia and Senegal. Thus the Security Council, which until the eruption in the Congo seemed almost to have withered away, may now find new life in Africa.

Finally, the outside world can help West Africa by insisting on judging Africans by the same standards as other people. This is because the relations which now exist between Africans and liberals in the rest of the world are somewhat unbalanced. Africans, like Asians or Latin Americans, tend to take a holier-than-thou attitude toward Europe and North America, which are freely criticized for their shortcomings. Indeed, in recent months in the United Nations, the African bloc has tended to take a holier-than-thou attitude even toward the Asians and the Latin Americans, which is quite an achievement. On the other hand, liberals in Europe and America tend to be mealy-mouthed about what is going on in West Africa, as if to say that an African nationalist can do no wrong. This ignores the fact that African nationalists do not think alike. Some are ruthless bosses, of the type of Huey Long. Others, like Olympio in Togoland, or Awolowo in Nigeria, are subtle and sophisticated liberal statesmen, who would bring distinction to political office in any country in the world. Such men are seeking to set new political standards in West Africa, and to create new and healthy political traditions. They are not helped when liberals in the outside world pay homage to men who behave like gangsters or keep silent in face of African atrocities.

The West has a long political tradition of a kind which West Africa is just learning, and criticism of African mistakes is an important form of aid. The best way to treat West Africans is to treat them as equals, recognizing that some are good and some bad, some are highly educated while others are illiterate, some have good sense while others are silly—in short that they are just like other people, neither better nor worse. The unequal treatment of the past underlies most of the current tensions; in the same way a friendly and helping hand now can set West Africa on a firm road to happiness and prosperity.

B. The Emergence of the American Negro

Ralph J. Bunche

To the individual, the close tension is likely to loom more ominously than that which is remote, or appears to be so. It has often been said, and rightly, that the rivalries and conflicts which create the taut political tensions between the two worlds commonly described as "East" and "West" or "Communist" and "free," should be our major concerns, as posing the greatest danger to world peace. It is urged, likewise, that the wide and ever-widening gap between the developed and underdeveloped peoples is a source of threatening tension. But, for example, the Negro in the American South, or really anywhere in the country, engaged in the climactic struggle for full equality, and the white Americans who resist this group effort to advance, are not likely to see it that way. For them, there are no greater tensions than those in the midst of which they live and which, indeed, they themselves create. For most of them, doubtless, the tensions of a summit meeting enjoy only secondary priority.

That is why I elect to approach the question of tensions from the standpoint of the individual—his attitudes as directly contributory to tension and his immediate responsibility for doing something about it.

Whatever and wherever the tension, it is the attitudes, suspicions, fears, and other emotions, spontaneous or propaganda-inspired, informed or misguided, of the individual, expressed in the mass, which are ultimately culpable. It follows that reduction in the intensity of any world tension would require a significant change in the attitudes of peoples as well as governments, the two processes, of course, being directly interrelated.

Indeed, in the world of today, all of the major tensions are interrelated. There is, for instance, our American problem of race relations. There is throughout the world a common reaction to racial repression, the most insidious—and senseless—of society's maladies, and quite possibly the most dangerous, insofar as it poses an unpredictable emotional factor in all peace calculations.

2

To its great credit, the United Nations, from its beginning, has recognized the fundamental and urgent nature of the problem of race relations, has stood firmly for the principles of equality among peoples, of human rights and human dignity, and has strongly opposed practices of racial discrimination anywhere in the world. This, indeed, is a major reason why many people have confidence in the United Nations.

Problems of race relations within national borders today inescapably have international significance and impact. This is true, of course, of the American version of the problem. It could not be otherwise, naturally, in a world whose people are preponderantly nonwhite and acutely sensitive to prejudice; in a world in which colonialism, though expiring, does so stubbornly in some places; in a world including the emerging continent of Africa.

The American problem illustrates particularly well the role of individuals in the perpetuation of a tension situation. The law of the land, expressed in the Constitution, in national legislation, and in decisions of the Federal Courts, stands for equality and is antidiscriminatory. Considerable progress toward elimination of racial discrimination has been made, especially in the postwar years. But the practice of discrimination continues as the basic design of relations between the races in the South, and to considerable extent all over the country. For this is a national, not a sectional problem. This condition persists because, in the North as well as the South, the attitudes of many people of the majority ethnic group are determined by prejudice in varying degrees of intensity based on ignorance, fear, custom, and rigid unreason.

Being on one side of the fence—for I am vigorously and unabashedly a partisan of the equalitarian cause of my group, although I hope, with calmness and reason—I have often wondered about the thinking of the white citizen on the other side who opposes my view. What really goes on in his mind and determines his attitude?

Does the white citizen who takes such a fierce stand against integration in the schools permit himself to look at places where it has always existed or has recently occurred in order to check on the validity of his fears? What is it that will permit him to stand shoulder to shoulder with Negroes in an elevator or ride side by side with them in an interstate train, bus, or plane, and object to doing so in a local bus or tram? What is it that is in his mind when he mingles freely with Negro shoppers all over a store but objects to one sitting on a stool at the same lunch counter with him in the same store? Is he really insincere in his acclaim of democracy? Does he never weigh the costs to his country and himself of racial strife? Does he really object to the Negro citizen as an American? Clearly, he does not, for he expects him to pay taxes, to fight for his country, and to assume all the other obligations of citizenship on the same basis as every other citizen. Or is it that the white citizen simply resists change? In this context, questions without end could be asked, but reason would never spawn answers to them.

I can speak more confidently about the attitude of the Negro American. Every one of us understands that the solution of the American race problem is not at all easy, that for many white fellow citizens, in the South particularly, the idea of change in the status of the Negro causes emotional disturbance, grave concern, and creates delicate problems of adjustment. But while the Negro recognizes this as an obstacle to change he insists that it cannot justify the perpetuation of serious social injustices. And he knows also that the nation's growth and maturity depend upon change and upon the advancement of all of its people, and that difficulties and disruptions are an inevitable by-product of any process of social and economic change.

The Negro demands equality, and while this requires a change in his status it embraces no special position or privilege for him. All that is at issue is that the individual Negro citizen be enabled to find his own level in society on the same basis as any other citizen—that of merit and not of color.

This is the crux of the problem of race relation tensions in America. The Negro seeks to escape only from socially imposed handicaps of race. He is not trying to get away from his ancestry. He is only trying to get rid of a penalty for having a different skin color. I am confident that I reflect accurately the views of virtually all Negro Americans when I say that I am proud of my ancestry, just as I am proud of my nationality. I ask only that the one be as much respected as the other. Difficult as the road ahead may be, the Negro is certain that he will before too long achieve his goal of full stature as an American citizen. Attitudes of people change, more readily, in fact, than it was once thought they could.

The American Negro knows, as every thinking and objective person must know, that it is not possible to be a good American and to be discriminated against at the same time, for whatever reasons, because this means not only loss of economic opportunity, but inferior education, and above all that denial of dignity which inevitably accompanies enforced segregation. In some places it still means disenfranchisement.

3

It will soon be a century since Emancipation, and that is more than half the age of the American nation; a long time, especially when measured in terms of the lives and aspirations and the lost opportunities of millions of individuals—about one-tenth of our population.

There have been some recent developments in the South which have been shocking to some people and grossly misread by others. It is, to be sure, unfortunate that such manifestations as the sit-down demonstrations have had to take place. But they are as inevitable as they are logical and justified. They are an expression of the utter dissatisfaction and impatience of the Negro in the South, and particularly the young Negro, with the slow pace of progress in the elimination of the material burdens and the intolerable humiliations of racial discrimination. These demonstrations have been spontaneous and it is a shameless slur against the courage and the honor of these heroic young people who engage in them for anyone to suggest that they are inspired or misled by sinister forces from outside their communities. They know what their privileges and rights are and they are determined to achieve them by every legal means. They would scarcely be worthy of them were they unwilling to do so. It is, I think, the finest tribute to the human species that, as history has often recorded, a time may be reached in the thinking of individuals when insistence on human dignity, when the compelling demand for respect, when a sheer sense of justice, boils up so fiercely inside them that direct action must and will be taken, whatever the risk.

For the tension resulting from this sort of problem of human relations, in our own country or wherever, there is but one remedy: equality through complete elimination of practices of discrimination. Here certainly is one source of tension which each of us, as individuals, can do something about—more, in the long run, I suspect, than governments; more, indeed, than could be done at any summit. This is a sphere in which no one of us ever does as much as he could do; in which the most earnestly converted may always do more. The individual—the most exalted and the humblest—is here confronted squarely with the challenge to convert good words, even good will, into good acts. Dare we truly ask ourselves: how do we each day by *all* our brothers?

SCIENCE: THE ONLY COMMON ENTERPRISE?

Eugene Rabinowitch

The scientific and technical knowledge of our time does not belong to a limited part of humanity—to any particular race, people, state, or political system. It has become a treasury of mankind as a whole, laid down in libraries in Tokyo, Rio de Janeiro, and New Delhi not less exhaustively than in those of Paris, Washington, London, and Leningrad. Men of all continents are its living carriers. A world-wide conflagration would be needed to consume its record. Nothing short of decimation of all mankind could break its living tradition.

Some will object that in our time the tenets of the world's religions and philosophies, the teachings of the world's economists and political scientists, the works of artists and the deeds of political leaders, also are preserved for posterity through what Ashby has called "the second channel of human inheritance"—the printed word. But it is conceivable that any one (or all) of them may disappear in the future. The parliamentary democracy and the party dictatorship, the realistic and the abstract art, the opera and the symphonic music, all these may conceivably become history at some future time, and be replaced by something not necessarily better, but different, carried on by biologically more successful sections of the human race. This is not true of science. It is the only truly common enterprise of mankind. Whatever fraction of humanity may become dominant in some future time, it will carry with it the same scientific tradition.

In ancient civilizations, science was often part of an esoteric culture, restricted to a priesthood, and jealously guarded from the noninitiated, native or alien. Modern science, on the other hand, has, since the Renaissance, adopted free dissemination of knowledge as its basic rule of conduct. Perhaps the greatest difference betwen alchemy and chemistry was that alchemists worked in secrecy, thus deepening and perpetuating their errors; while chemists have sought from the beginning to spread information about their discoveries, exposing them to critical scrutiny and thereby tending to eliminate error. Modern science is deeply aware that scientific error thrives on secrecy, while scientific truth flourishes in the open market. It has found its key to steady and sound progress in continuous subjection of all scientific findings to critical analysis by fellow scientists all over the world. In the years following World War II, the American as well as the Soviet government attempted to keep certain areas of science a national monopoly, and share them only with trusted allies. The era of secrecy is not yet over; but political secrecy is already revealed as largely irrelevant to the main stream of the world-wide scientific progress.

There have been times in modern history when scientific cooperation was maintained between nations even while they were at war, as between English and French scientists at the time of the Napoleonic Wars. The emergence, in our era, of states claiming domination over the whole material and spiritual life of their peoples, posed a challenge to this tradition of a supranational community of scientists. At the beginning of the Franco-Prussian War, in 1870, prominent German chemists indulged in boastful attacks on supposedly inferior French science, causing the Russian Academy of Sciences to deplore unwarranted intrusion of nationalism into the world of science. Even worse things happened in 1914, at the beginning of World War I, when some prominent scientists joined the infamous manifesto of German intellectuals proclaiming the superiority of German civilization, and pledged their support to the German armed power as incarnation of the German spirit.

Between the two World Wars, nationalism in science was carried *ad absurdum* in Communist Russia and Hitlerite Germany. In Moscow, proletarian science was proclaimed superior to bourgeois science; the dialectic-materialist science of Soviet Russia was declared to be the only truly scientific one, and the "idealist" science of the West was denounced as full of errors. In the resulting isolation, error became protected and scientific truth slighted. Relativity and quantum mechanics (in particular, the new concept of causality in atomic physics) were chastised as contrary to the teachings of Engels and Lenin; the basic concepts of genetics were forcibly evicted from biology. In Germany, analogous attempts to discredit "Semitic" science and to glorify Aryan science, went even further. Not only were Jewish professors dismissed and exiled, but the fundamental theories of modern physics were rejected as alien to the Northern spirit, and therefore invalid. A swarm of cranks—alchemists, astrologists, adherents of the "ice theory" of the universe—clamored for, and received, support from the Nazi government even more readily than did legitimate scientists. This further weakened German science, already crippled by the elimination of its strong Jewish contingent—of Albert Einstein, Max Born, Otto Stern, James Franck, Hans Bethe, and many, many others of the first rank, whose exodus revitalized science in Britain and America.

2

In the Soviet Union, the crest of chauvinism in science came after the war. Throughout the 1920's and early 1930's, the channels of communication between Soviet science and the West remained open. Russian scientists were the only individuals in Russia permitted to visit Europe, occasionally even to spend several months in Western laboratories; Western scientists were encouraged to come to Russia. The ideological pressure of conformity remained relatively weak in physical sciences; but biology was, from the beginning, seriously exposed.

Attacks on genetics were started by Lysenko in the late 1920's; his ideological mentors proclaimed that Mendelian genetics was contrary to the dialectical materialism. Lysenko's hour of triumph came, however, when Russian chauvinism, fostered by Stalin during the war, was added to ideological dogmatism. Lysenko identified himself, not only with dialectical materialism, but also with the masters of Russian biology in the prerevolutionary era—the educated Westerner, Timiriazev, and the self-taught scientist, Michurin. Lysenko proclaimed himself heir to their tradition, and riding the double wave of fanatic dogmatism and chauvinism, he managed to extend his influence over a large part of biological science in Russia. Genetics was completely destroyed; inroads were made also into the teaching and research in embryology, physiology, and other biological disciplines.

The crest of this wave of obscurantism was reached by the time of Stalin's death. Since then it has subsided, but as yet not entirely. Lysenko still has powerful friends in the Central Committee of the Communist party and maintains a dominant position in the Academy of Agricultural Sciences and many agricultural research stations. Outspoken criticism of his personality and teachings on the pages of some biological journals published by the Soviet Academy of Sciences was denounced by no less an authority than Khrushchev himself, and led, in 1959, to the replacement of the editors, and changes in the personnel of the Biology Division of the Academy of Sciences. This time, however, no personal punishments were meted out to the enemies of Lysenko, and they seem to continue unhampered in their research and teaching. The geneticists still have a hard time reemerging from oblivion; genetic research in the Soviet Union, which once, in the late 1930's, had gotten off to a brilliant start, has not been able by 1960 to contribute again significantly to the world-wide progress of this science, which in the meantime has become central to our understanding of life. The plan of the new "Science Town" near Novosibirsk in Siberia does include an institute devoted to genetics, under the directorship of Dubinin, the foremost Russian geneticist; but it may be not accidental that the development of genetics in Russia has been relegated to this faraway corner of the country.

It is, however, a sign of Russia's turning away from dogmatic isolationism in science that, even when the Soviet authorities protect Lysenko and his school from attacks by "Westernized" biologists, they do this in the name of freedom of science. The official line, laid down by the Communist leadership, says: let every trend in science show what it can achieve, particularly in the way of practical advancement of agriculture; let all scientists work together and eliminate their errors by cooperative research. Unfortunately, no serious scientist can cooperate fruitfully with a self-willed ignoramus such as Lysenko, who tells American visitors that controlled experiments are inventions of the decadent West. ("Why make errors at all?" he says when asked about the probable error in his findings.) He keeps his standing with the Soviet government by continuous promises of spectacular developments in plant growing, and more recently in animal breeding—advances which escape independent control because of uncritical and secretive methodology.

Nationalism, too, has had but slight effect on the progress of physical sciences in Russia. With official encouragement, the tendency to quote Russian work out of proportion to its relative value in a given field has become prevalent in the Soviet scientific literature; the popular science journals through which science trickles down to the general readership make hardly any mention at all of the achievements of foreign science or technology—unless they occur in China or a "popular democracy." However, this is only a superficial protective coloring. The truly important Russian physicists and chemists of today grew up in the schools of first-class pre-revolutionary scientists, men such as Joffe, Frumkin, Frenkel, Vavilov, Skobeltzyn, or Zelinsky, who transmitted to them the respect for the achievements of the giants of modern physics and chemistry, from Boyle and Lavoisier, through the Curies and Rutherford, to Bohr, Heisenberg, and Fermi, and implanted in them the understanding of the organic unity of the scientific progress in all parts of the world. When the dams of isolationism in nuclear science broke in 1955, at the first Atoms for Peace Conference in Geneva, American participants were struck by the reverence with which young Russian scientists met their famous Western colleagues; it was obviously a great event in their lives to have personally encountered Hahn and Cockcroft, Rabi, and von Laue, and many others whose names they have revered from their college days; and they showed some of this respectful attitude also toward the younger American pioneers in nuclear science.

The present generation of Russian scientists, particularly those in the physical sciences, carries very little inheritance of dogmatic and nationalistic isolationism. They bring their feeling of solidarity with Western scientists to enthusiastic expression whenever they feel themselves free to do so—occasions which have become increasingly frequent in recent years. Without this cosmopolitan attitude (a complimentary adjective for a scientist, however opprobrious the Soviet propaganda has tried to make it) Russian physical science could not have developed as rapidly and successfully as it did in recent years.

Historians, economists, and sociologists who have recently visited the Soviet Union have been struck by the smug belief of their Soviet colleagues in exclusive possession of a kind of revealed truth and an ability to produce, on the spot, final answers to all difficult questions; as well as by their ignorance of Western developments in the areas in which they were supposed to be experts. No such arrogance—or ignorance—can exist among scientists. The standards on which achievements in science are measured are the same in

Russia and in the West; what is true for a Western physicist or chemist is also true for his Russian or Chinese colleague; and the latter cannot but be aware of the fact that the majority of the most important achievements in their fields have originated, and still originate, in the West—in England, Denmark, and Holland, in Sweden, France, Germany, and more and more often in recent decades, in the United States.

Politicians and journalists may believe (and convince the general public) that the Russian firsts in missilry and space travel are evidence of Russian science being ahead of that of the rest of the world; but the Russian scientists themselves, including those responsible for the Sputniks and the Luniks, know well what they owe to the West. They also know that spectacular technological deeds are not the most important standards by which to measure the state of science in a country; and, most importantly, they know as we do that the whole question of relative standing of different countries in science has little meaning.

Science is an international effort, and a scientific discovery gives no special credit, and—in the long run—brings no more advantage to the country where it has been made than it does to all other countries of sufficient technological capacity and open-mindedness to be able to assimilate and exploit it. Nations can put different emphases on practical applications of certain scientific discoveries; and can thus achieve leadership in one or the other of them, be it long-range rocketry, automation, or combating certain diseases. But even in such selected areas, leadership is by necessity temporary— the Russians rapidly caught up with the American breakthrough in nuclear weapons and nuclear energy; the Americans are catching up with the Soviet breakthrough in the building of high-power rockets; the Ceylonese have learned how to eradicate malaria; the Africans how to fight sleeping sickness.

In our time, technological innovation moves closer and closer to scientific discovery, and the previously valid concept of separate technological civilizations in different parts of the world fades away; progress in technology becomes as much of a single, world-wide process as the world development of science has been since the Renaissance. The steam engine, the cotton gin, and the mechanical reaper were discovered not by scientists, but by practical inventors; the use of such devices could be restricted for some time to the country of their invention, giving it great economic benefits. In our time, an attempt to keep nuclear technology a monopoly of the West collapsed within a couple of years (as American scientists predicted it would); close relationship of this technology to fundamental science made all hope to keep it out of the reach of the Russians foolish and futile.

By the force of events, we are now brought to consider the advisability of pooling national efforts in space technology instead of continuing indefinitely our own competitive program; after having been frustrated in our original intent to monopolize all nuclear power developments in a UN agency, we are haltingly moving toward an international program of atomic energy development for industrial purposes. In applied, as distinct from fundamental, science, Soviet isolationism may be more difficult to overcome, as was demonstrated in UN negotiations on the Baruch Plan. But the objective facts of the situation are such that even the doctrinaire Soviet technological planners cannot indefinitely deny that the development of large-scale scientific technology is not fundamentally different in countries with different economic systems, and often calls for cooperative, supranational effort.

It cannot be said that all is now sweetness and light between Russian and Western science. There remain areas of direct ideological pressure, where Communist party philosophers still try to deduce scientific truth not from the findings of science itself, but from the tenets of dialectical materialism. There also persists a general pretense that even if the methods and content of science developments in the non-Communist West and in the Communist East may be essentially the same, they serve different masters. Western science, according to this propaganda, serves the selfish interests of capitalists, while Communist science serves the people —represented, of course, by the party. In the West, it is said, science is encouraged only to the extent to which it increases the profits of members of the ruling class; in the East it is supported unreservedly, because its progress ultimately devolves to the benefit of the people as a whole.

There is, unfortunately, just enough truth in the comparison of the somewhat halting support science receives in America (and even more so in most European countries) with the privileged position in which science finds itself in the allocation of national resources in the Communist countries, to make this fable plausible to many Russian scientists. This, however, does not weaken their solidarity with the scientists of the West; but it does create a slightly condescending attitude in pupils who have acquired high social and economic status, toward a respected teacher who still labors under cramped conditions and with inadequate economic support.

In annual reviews of the state of Soviet science, regularly prepared by the Soviet Academy President, the chemist Nesmeyanov, and his Vice President, also a chemist, Topchiev, this difference is exploited to the full. The Western scientists are made to appear in such official presentations as friends, and every contact with them is mentioned with satisfaction; but they are also represented as working against their better judgment and in conflict with their true feelings, for the benefit of capitalists; while the Soviet scientists are said to live in felicitous harmony with their Communist leaders whose aspirations for the well-being of all people they wholeheartedly share.

It is an open question to what extent this misrepresentation of the role of the scientists in the libertarian societies of the West is accepted unquestionably by the scientific élite of Soviet Russia. Their contacts with their western colleagues confirm that the economic position of scientists, relative to the general standard of living, is less advantageous in the West than in their Communist society. American scientists, inquiring about the sources of funds for the large scientific projects in the Soviet Union—the cyclotrons, the nuclear reactors, the space rockets—are likely to receive the somewhat condescending answer, "We just tell the government what we need and we get it." On the other hand, however, Russian scientists are fully aware of—and envious of—the professional freedom of their Western colleagues; freedom from interference in the choice of research, from pressure for participation in practical programs and from lip service to an official ideology; freedom to travel all over the world—and above all, freedom from terror, which the Soviet scientists, together with all others in Russia, have barely escaped and fervently hope will never face again.

Even if many, perhaps the majority, of Russian scientists now identify themselves with the economic and cultural aims of the Soviet leadership, and feel pride in their contributions to the success of these efforts, this identification does not involve feelings of antagonism toward the scientists of the West, or of a superiority resulting from the possession of better philosophical equipment. With few exceptions, Russian scientists do not believe in the infallibility of dialectic materialism as the basis of scientific progress (as they are continuously told by their leaders, including the top brass of the Academy of Sciences). In fact, they are inclined to consider this philosophy as irrelevant to their scientific work.

The Russian scientists know well that the boldest progress in science has been achieved when there was freedom to question all established truths—as their own Lobachevsky has questioned the principles of Euclidian geometry, as Einstein has questioned the universally accepted concepts of time and space, as the creators of quantum mechanics have questioned the continuity of the world in space, and its strict causality in time. If, as a precautionary habit, they pay homage to the Communist leadership, they do it in the same way in which their medieval predecessors dedicated their treatises to the monarchs or aristocrats on whose support they were dependent; if they praise dialectical materialism, they do it in the same perfunctory way in which earlier scientists made obeisance to the then established religions.

3

What does the homogeneity of the scientific community of the world, the common language its members speak, even in countries otherwise separated by allegiance to different ideologies, mean for the world today? One thing is certain: it means more than it has ever meant before. In the past, scientists tended to share not only their scientific attitudes, but also the same liberal attitudes toward political and economic questions; while in our time, they are widely divided in this respect. Nevertheless, their affinities now count more than their disagreements. This is so, in the first place, because science has become a much more important part of national life; and in the second place, because mutual alienation of nations has reached a new pitch, making every bridge of understanding between them more important than ever.

In the nineteenth century, one could believe that the liberal civilization of Western Europe was on the way toward becoming a universal civilization of mankind. The less progressive countries were fully anticipated to advance, one by one, to full partnership in it; and the colonial people were vaguely expected to reach the same status in some indefinite future. In our time, the concepts and ideals of Western democracy and secular political philosophy are still spreading through the world, as evidenced by the adoption of democratic forms of new Asian and African nations from Japan to Nigeria, and in the secularization of previously theocratic societies (although Arabia, Pakistan, and Indonesia show a stubborn Moslem resistance to the latter change). But a new and radically different economic ideology has arisen in our time—a system that substitutes central economic planning for the release of unfettered individual initiative as the mainspring of economic progress, and adopts party dictatorship instead of parliamentary democracy as the proper instrument of political power. The relative success of this system is being abetted by technological progress, which has made free market competition illusory in many important areas of economic and technical endeavor.

Since the two World Wars, the new concept of good society has been in strong competition with the older libertarian idea for the allegiance of most countries of Europe; as far as its economic beliefs are concerned, it came near to displacing it in England, the home of economic liberalism; it gained violent victory in Russia and China, and is now competing for the minds of the under-developed countries. The latter have become free from colonial tutelage much sooner than was expected only a few years ago; they are striving to lift themselves by the bootstraps, and see great advantages in a centrally organized effort to utilize modern scientific technology. In the controversy between these two systems, the new one has proclaimed a fanatic belief in its inevitable ultimate victory; and this has created on the other side a legitimate revulsion, no less intense than that which the English mercantile aristocracy once had felt against the egalitarian terror of the French Revolution. The new ideological struggle has become superimposed, throughout the world, on traditional power rivalries, religious conflicts, and clashes of economic interests. Of the historical reasons for war, only dynastic controversies have been largely eliminated; and even they still linger in the Middle East.

Thus, the world is now further from fundamental unity than it seemed to be a hundred and fifty years ago. But science, the force that has made the threat of war so overwhelmingly terrible, also offers, for the first time in history, a reasonable prospect for a common enterprise of all nations, for a program of cooperation which could benefit all of them irrespective of their political, ideological, economic, or religious allegiances: a program creating new wealth, instead of fighting for the distribution of the limited existing wealth.

The conflict between the newly-born spirit of rational, world-wide scientific cooperation, and the traditional prescientific spirit of invidious competition and power conflict, exacerbated a thousandfold by the acquisition of scientific weapons, is the tragic dilemma of our time. It is reflected in such local situations as those that exist between India and Pakistan, or between Israel and Syria.

A rational program which would benefit both sides would be common development of the power and irrigation potentials of the rivers Indus and Jordan; but this mutually profitable solution is frustrated by the traditional attitudes, which refuse to admit that anything good for one side could also be good for the other.

4

International cooperation in science is an old story. The International Union of Chemical Societies, the International Astronomical Union, and other similar bodies are long-established organizations. Long before the war, international scientific meetings were held regularly, and attended by individuals from all countries, including the Soviet Union. However, the strength of these scientific ties has been, in the past, negligible in comparison with the forces which drove nations apart. The relation was not too different from that in the international labor movement, where the First and Second Socialist International meekly disintegrated at the outbreak of a war between European nations, despite the assertions of socialist ideologists that the proletariat has no fatherland, and that its only loyalty is to the laboring classes of the world. In the same way, the mutual loyalties of scientists of different countries were submerged when military conflicts broke out between their nations.

Nobody would be so unrealistic as to assert that the new international links in science, forged since the return of the Russian scientists to the international fold at the 1955 Atoms for Peace Conference at Geneva, and strengthened since by increasingly numerous international conferences and multiplying mutual visits, are strong enough to withstand a major political crisis. However, in some respects these links are stronger than those that had existed in the past. This is so because science has become a much

more important factor in national and international life, and because collaboration in science has begun to extend to major technological enterprises.

The international meteorological service has long been just about
the only form of scientific collaboration which had considerable
practical importance. Two international meteorological years were
held long before the war, and have served as prototypes for the
recent International Geophysical Year. The IGY became, however, a much more ambitious world-wide scientific enterprise,
aimed at broadening and deepening the knowledge of the planet,
whose surface the nations have divided among themselves, but
whose atmosphere defied division into "national air masses," and
whose hydrosphere has enjoyed international status for a century.
In the International Geophysical Year, units of the fleets and air
forces of individual nations were pressed into the service of science;
together with astronomical and geophysical research institutions
they vied in gathering information about the earth and its liquid
and gaseous envelopes. As part of these cooperative efforts, the
first Soviet and American satellites were launched. The press and
the public opinions of the world may look upon these exploits as
purely national achievements; but it should not be forgotten
that most of those responsible for them did consider them,
their contributions to an international program, undertaken for
the benefit of all humanity.

The great success of the International Geophysical Year—it will
take years to work up the enormous experimental material ac-
cumulated during its eighteen months—has encouraged an indefinite extension of many of its activities on an international basis;
it has also stimulated a search for other areas, in which analogous
cooperative programs would be possible and desirable. We are
certain to see such projects multiply and become a permanent
aspect of international life. Whether an International Medical
Year will soon materialize or not, cooperation in medical research,
human and animal epidemiology, and preventive medicine, is

bound to grow under the auspices of the UN and other organizations. The proposal for an International Medical Year, introduced jointly by the United States and the USSR, was defeated in a UN committee by the majority of smaller nations, who felt that the available means can be used more effectively in other ways—a striking illustration of the way which ideological alignments are broken when attention is turned to problems of science and technology.

The Soviet Union has proposed international pooling of research efforts in the field of thermonuclear energy production; the United States has championed—and the Soviet Union has now accepted—a similar pooling of efforts in space research. Enormous funds are now being invested by individual nations in nuclear and space research, and the benefits which may accrue to all of them from a successful cooperative effort in these fields are incalculable. A crowning glory—economical production of thermonuclear power—would remove once and for all the haunting specter of the ultimate decay of mankind caused by the exhaustion of fossil (chemical or nuclear) fuels.

Perhaps the most significant development of recent years has been the extension of competition between the two camps now existing in the world, from the perfection of weapons (an area of technology in which no common interest exists between the competitors) to technical assistance to underdeveloped nations (an area where competition willy-nilly leads to cooperation, because it is directed at the common primary aim of raising the technical potential of a backward nation). The effect on the economy of India of a steel mill built with Soviet assistance will be essentially that of a steel mill built with American assistance. Only if such assistance were to become quite one-sided could the technical and psychological involvement of the recipient with the donor nation lead to affiliation with one side in the bipolar world; if both sides contribute to the advancement, its practical success can mean the end of a dangerous stagnation and the beginning of a hopeful advance, at the end of which a now underdeveloped nation will be able to determine its own future without the pressure of popular despair.

The West can believe, with good reason, that under these conditions no nation will voluntarily choose Communist dictatorship in preference to systems affording more freedom to the individual (and this hope is strengthened by the fact that none has chosen so in the past). The East may be equally convinced that, in the foreseeable future, the advantages of an orderly, centralized, planned society over the "anarchic" capitalist way of life, will have become so obvious as to make the choice in its favor inevitable. What matters in the present juncture is that the immediate purposes of both sides in this area are becoming parallel and not antagonistic. This, too, is the consequence of the scientific revolution. Without this revolution, the Communist leadership would have continued placing its hope on the pauperization and despair of colonial masses, deprived of their share of natural wealth by colonial exploitation. The technological revolution made it clear, however, that the key to progress lies not in changing the system of distribution of the existing wealth, but in greater production of new wealth, and that if the Communist leadership would stand aside in the drive for increased production in underdeveloped countries, others will carry it on to success.

The development of science thus creates, de facto, a world-wide community of constructive effort, and this new phenomenon becomes superimposed upon the age-old—and still very real—international struggle for power, in which the supreme good for one nation often is the supreme evil for another nation, as the destruction of Israel appears as supreme good to the Arab states. We thus live in an exciting, dual world, in which international life proceeds on two levels: the level of traditional power competition which in history has always led to climaxes of naked violence, and the level of quickening international collaboration.

To sum up, the progress of science in our time has brought about two things of great relevance to the world situation: it has made the consequences of continued power policy too terrible to contemplate, and has given new, realistic meaning to the old dream of an international community. The future of mankind depends on which of the two types of international intercourse will prove to be more viable.

5

Much of what is written these days on science and world tensions deals only with the reduction of secrecy in scientific publication, free exchange of scientific literature, free travel of scientists to international meetings—in short, the restoration of the state of professional openness in world science which had existed before 1914, and was largely, but not completely, restored also between the two World Wars. Such a liberalization is, of course, important to permit the cohesive force of scientific intercourse and collaboration to exert its unifying influence. But much more than freedom of professional contacts is at issue.

Much of the old openness in the professional sphere has in fact been restored already. Scientists themselves have been responsible for revealing to the public, particularly in the United States, the senselessness and futility of attempts to keep advances in basic science secret. Their protest has been largely successful. Most fundamental research, even in nuclear physics, has by now been "declassified," not only in the United States and Europe, but, by and large, in the Soviet Union. In this way, the most paralyzing effect of secrecy—the uncertainty in the mind of independent scientists who may want to tackle a certain problem, as to what has already been done in this field, has been lifted. Even in the applied fields of nuclear and thermonuclear reactor development, the most important cards are now on the table, face up. There are, of course, certain fields which remain closed, such as rocket fuel research, studies of the behavior of materials at high temperature and under high stress related to rocket technology, studies of the biological properties of compounds potentially useful in chemical warfare, and so on. The world would be better off if all this information were released for publication in professioinal journals, but the remaining secrecy has ceased to be a major block to international exchange of ideas.

Personal communication—traveling to international conferences, visiting foreign laboratories, and debating matters of common interest personally or by mail—is as yet in poorer shape. Bureaucratic and linguistic handicaps still stand in the way. Instead of blanket permission to scientists to travel to international meetings and to visit laboratories where research in kindred subjects is carried out, American and Soviet bureaucracies have contrived cumbersome bilateral "exchanges"—two American astrophysicists visiting Soviet observatories in exchange for two Soviet astrophysicists visiting similar American institutions, and other such arrangements. A matching game has developed which takes the time of government officials and of scientists, leads to unnecessary delay, and often ends in the abandonment of traveling plans. Apparently the Soviet Union still has misgivings about permitting its individual scientists to travel in foreign countries, not to speak of spending enough time in foreign laboratories to carry out significant research (even a year's stay is often insufficient to assimilate and develop a new experimental technique!); while the American government cannot be persuaded that letting Russian scientists work in our laboratories means not a one-sided profit for the Soviet Union's scientific effort, but mutual profit for both sides. Receiving such visits can often bring as much broadening of our knowledge of Soviet research as would a visit of our scientists to a Soviet laboratory. One hopes that bureaucratic one-for-one exchanges of scientists will soon be replaced by a smoothing of the paths for all individual scientists who may want to become acquainted with their colleagues and their laboratories in other countries. We stand to gain even if this should mean fifty Russian scientists visiting America for only ten American scientists going to Russia.

It would be to our advantage, in fact, to let in all Soviet scientists who may want to come to the United States; and even to provide funds for their travel and stay here, since shortage of dollars seems to be a very real barrier in the path of scientific travel out of the Soviet Union, Poland, Yugoslavia, and other countries of Eastern Europe.

In addition to the strait jacket of a bureaucratic "barter," the international communication between scientists is handicapped by the language barrier. This, too, is being gradually overcome. For the time being, in this country, it occurs only in small part by an increase in the linguistic capacities of American scientists, and mostly by the more expensive and less satisfactory procedure of wholesale translation of scientific literature, including all the most important scientific journals, from Russian into English (and similar systematic translation of English scientific literature into Russian in the Soviet Union). In any case, by now no American scientist can justify a lack of acquaintance with important work in his field, carried out in the Soviet Union, by his inability to read Russian.

It has been argued—for example, by Szilard and by Melman and his associates in the Columbia study on disarmament controls— that extensive travel of scientists between the East and the West could provide a most effective control over the carrying out of disarmament treaties. Since, they argued, no significant weapon development appears possible in our time without the participation of a considerable group of scientists, the existence of a clandestine development is likely to leak out, if extensive conversations between scientists of different countries were to be permitted or even encouraged. The mere disappearance of a certain number of important scientists from international traffic would be a hint of their participation in a secret military project.

Mixing international intercourse in science with the search for illegal activities is not a sound idea. The combination of scientific visits with inspection trips, and of scientific conversations between colleagues with gathering of intelligence information, is neither desirable nor effective. The only legitimate purpose of international communication in science is the strengthening of the world community based on mutual trust—and trust between nations must be achieved by more than mutual policing. While the latter is necessary, it should be strictly limited, and kept apart from friendly intercourse.

Apparatus for the monitoring of disarmament agreements, for example, such as the seismic stations provided in the present plans for a nuclear test ban, should not be disguised as organs of international scientific cooperation, however desirable this may appear at first sight. Perhaps later, when mutual trust is much improved and monitoring has become a dull routine, such stations could be given also more interesting research assignments; but as of now, mixing intelligence aims with scientific intercourse between the West and the East would be a grave error.

Furthermore, "inspection through friendly chats" is not an efficient procedure. Of course, during the war, the existence of the atom bomb project in the United States could be easily deduced from the disappearance of a large number of scientists, particularly nuclear physicists, into remote laboratories; but this was a unique episode. Development of nuclear weapons and of means of their delivery has now become a specialized activity, carried out by groups of scientists whose names are largely unknown to other scientists in their own country. Only a few outstanding and internationally known physicists are still involved in this activity. Teams necessary for its continuation could easily be formed—not only in Russia, but even in the United States—without wide knowledge by other scientists. Even quarterly Soviet-American conferences of nuclear scientists, in which half of the names of the American participants would be designated by the Russians and half of the names of the Soviet participants, by Americans (a clever device suggested by one American scientist), could not provide assurance that any clandestine development of nuclear weapons will not remain secret.

6

In different historical periods, different social groups have played a particularly important role in the definition of national values and aims, the education of the people, and the formation of national policies. Priests and prophets largely shaped Jewish history in Biblical times; generals and legislators laid the basis for Roman power, and impressed on Roman civilization their values and their methods of action. Mercantile captains of England molded much of the British national values and national policies in the era of classical liberalism; the philosophers of the enlightenment and their remote descendants, the revolutionists of the nineteenth and twentieth centuries, have affected the modes of life, the political views, and the historical fate of European nations and of the United States. In the last hundred and fifty years the Marxists have oversimplified this relationship by assigning to each historical period a single dominant economic class; they interpreted the attitudes and policies of each period as expressions of the material interests and self-serving ideology of this class; but we do not need to accept this oversimplified interpretation. The groups which have exercised predominant influence on the ideals and policies of nations have often been other than economic; their ideology has often shaped the economic attitudes of their time rather than being shaped by it.

In our time, science has become a new and important force in human affairs, on national as well as international levels. This calls for scientists as a social group to accept a greater share of responsibility in the development of national consciousness and the formation of national policies. In contrast to past eras, ours is an eclectic civilization, not dominated by the mentality of a single group. The legal profession, the organized religions, the mercantile class, the industrial leadership, the labor unions, all these groups have accepted their part of responsibility in political life; they all contribute to the definition of national values and the development of national policies. The new responsibility of scientists is to take their place in the national councils, and to help mold the consciousness of our people and their political behavior, to permit full use of the constructive possibilities of science and prevent the calamity of its misuse for destruction. One of the attributes of the scientific spirit, which is particularly significant and potentially useful in this connection, is its essentially cosmopolitan character. The concepts, aims, and methods common to scientists, under whatever political, economic, or ideological systems they may live, permit them to establish channels of communication and perhaps even to undertake coordinated action directed at the education of nations and their leaders as to the realities, necessities, and potentialities of the scientific revolution.

This new importance of science in international affairs is being slowly and grudgingly recognized by the more traditional bearers of influence and power both in the West and in the East. We cannot deal here with all the evidence of increasing participation of scientists in international political negotiations in official or semiofficial capacity—as delegates to the Geneva conferences on nuclear test bans and surprise attack (Professors Fist, Bethe, Panofsky, Fedorov, and many others), as negotiators on the international exchange of scientists (Bronk, Nesmeyanov), and in many other roles. The creation of the President's advisory committee on science (first with Professor Killian and then with Professor Kistiakovsky as chairman) has given scientists a growing influence on the long-range planning of American policies; the organization of similar advisory committees by political parties and individual presidential candidates, their increasing participation in hearings by congressional committees on defense and foreign policy—all these are symptoms that the increasing political relevance of scientific problems and scientific opinion in our time is being recognized by the administration and the legislature.

The arms race in nuclear and rocket weapons, which dominates the international scene, is after all a creation of science. Scientists, not military men, first took the initiative toward the development of the atom bomb in 1939; scientists and not the military initiated also the addition to the dreaded fission bomb of the apocalyptic fusion bomb. They initiated—first in Germany, then in Russia, and now also in America—the development of long-range rockets, and thus created arsenals of weapons which now make every city on the globe open to destruction in a matter of minutes from any other point on earth. Scientists first recognized the full implications of the discovery of nuclear fission for the national security of all countries, including the United States, and predicted the inevitability of a nuclear arms race in a divided world. They were also the first to call for international control of nuclear energy as the only means to prevent this race. When UN negotiations on this control became stranded on the rocks of traditional power politics, scientists first suggested the cessation of nuclear weapons tests, as a practically feasible step toward the abatement of the race. Scientists, not only in the United States, but also in the Soviet Union, "sold" the idea of test cessation to their governments. In the international conference of scientific experts in Geneva, two years ago, this proposal ceased to be one of the many topics of fruitless wrangling between the East and the West, and became a subject of concrete negotiations, in which both sides search for a mutually acceptable, adequate, technical way to a mutually agreed aim.

Test cessation in itself is not a very important matter; but it provides a good example of the invasion of international policies by essentially scientific problems, and of the necessity of bringing scientists to help in shaping national policies when such problems are brought into the foreground.

Without agreed coordination, Soviet scientists have been telling their government the same things about the destructive capacity of nuclear weapons, the catastrophic consequences of a nuclear war, and the questionable chances of developing effective defenses, as American scientists are telling the U.S. government. Their technical advice concerning the monitoring of a test ban (or other disarmament agreements) also is by necessity the same—these are scientific matters, and admit of only one scientifically sound answer. When the second conference of scientific experts in Geneva, held late last year, ended in disagreement, it was not for technical but for political reasons (on which we cannot dwell here); nevertheless, the scientific information contributed by the Americans and which the Russians were not permitted to consider in Geneva, found a quick way to the Soviet government. This is witnessed by Khrushchev's speech, in January, 1960, acknowledging the probable correctness of this information.

7

For the last three years, an attempt has been made to establish channels of communication between scientists of all countries, particularly between those of the West and of the Soviet Union, to exchange privately and informally their opinions on problems raised by the scientific revolution, and perhaps coordinate their activities in this area. These problems include not only the scientific arms race and the possibility of a scientific war (particularly the technical aspects of arms control and world security), but also the possibility of positive, constructive cooperation between scientists of the East and the West, and their general responsibility in our time.

This attempt led to five conferences—known as "Pugwash Conferences" after the place of the first meeting at Pugwash, Nova Scotia—in three years.

The rule of the Pugwash Conferences has been to issue no public statements except those adopted "practically unanimously," and to avoid pronouncement of general desiderata without contribution to public information and thinking on the subject. After initial astonishment, the Soviet scientists gradually recognized the desirability of conferences of this unusual type, and have given the idea considerable publicity in their scientific press.

The Pugwash meetings—and the Pugwash-type conferences held elsewhere in the world—have demonstrated at least one thing of great importance: it is in unofficial discussion that the virtues of mutual understanding and common way of thinking of scientists of all political backgrounds has the best possibility of asserting itself. No doubt, their practical significance is as yet (and may always remain) small compared to the activities of scientists engaged in official negotiations or advising their governments. But private conversations can achieve certain things difficult of achievement in official conferences—a frank exploration of the situation, as it appears to the scientifically trained minds. They may even lead to a long-range, coordinated effort in public education, aimed at making the political world a fit place for man armed with the tools of modern science.

7

FULL PROMISE OF A
DISTRACTED WORLD

Adlai E. Stevenson

I want to question one or two of our attitudes and beliefs from which all our policies in the international field—all our strategies and plans, all our efforts to mitigate the tensions of our world— are in the last analysis derived.

My first query is this. Do we know, in the broadest sense, what we are trying to do with our foreign policy? And what relation does it bear to what we ought to be doing in the atomic age? We accept the fact that, every day, science is revolutionizing our environment. Space is conquered. Communication is instant. World-wide political forces—anticolonialism, antiracism, burning nationalism— operate across the old boundaries and often obliterate them. Even in less sensational ways, we are caught in a new web of international influences and commitments. Is not one reason for the new pressure on America's balance of payments the freedom with which producers and consumers alike now shop around the world, turning naturally to foreign suppliers when price and convenience dictate the choice?

In short, we are irreversibly part of a world-wide human community. But it is not a community that enjoys the structure or the safeguards of a civilized society. At home we live under law. We play our part in promoting the general welfare. We share some sense of national purpose. These are surely the minimum conditions of a truly civic life, or a life in society that deserves the name of human.

But all are lacking in our international world. Should not, therefore, the introduction of such fundamental institutions be the first aim of our world policy? Should we not at least attempt a political inventiveness which in some way matches the horrific inventiveness of our scientists? Can we tolerate a world in which everything changes—every measurement, every distance, every material prospect—and only civic life remains unchanged to founder in an environment for which it was never designed?

The main aims of our foreign policies by-pass this central issue. We do not pursue the general welfare. We pursue our separate national interests and hope that the selfish good of the part will add up—against the witness of all social history—to the wider good of the whole.

We don't urgently seek a world under law. Primarily we seek national security or, in simpler terms, to stop the Russians. As for policies which attempt to articulate some common purpose for a threatened humanity, they occasionally get a brief run in our rhetoric. But they don't occupy much of our planners' time.

So I would suggest that a first need in our international policies is to be clear about our fundamental aims. We are trying to construct a civilized world for the genus man. We are trying to create for the whole human family institutions, obligations, decencies, and traditions which will enable it—with planetary suicide in sight —to avoid disaster and build for itself a saner, comelier life on earth. This aim may appear one of high generality. But so are such phrases as "the defense of national interests," or "Lebensraum," or "the white man's burden," or any of the other catch phrases with which men have gone out with good conscience to plunder and maim their neighbors. Behind the generality "national security" lies the concrete misery of a thousand wars. At least the aim of living as neighbors under a common law, with mutual support and respect, is an ideal with less palpably lethal consequences for the human race.

A world under law entails essentially an end to the settlement of disputes by private violence. And this in the context of 1960 means, first of all, a dedicated, unshakable search for arms control. Here again I wonder whether some of our beliefs and stereotypes are not hampering the energy of our search. We are bargaining with a tough and resourceful adversary. Nothing will be given away. Sentiment will not enter in. The only basis for negotiation is certainly to match strength for strength, concession for concession, and never to suggest for a moment that the Russians can have something for nothing in the field of security. Nobody has improved on Churchill's definition of our posture at the bargaining table: "We arm to parley." Heaven help us if we don't.

But equally, we aim to parley; to parley is the objective, for it is the only way to peace open to either side. Times have changed since diplomats could sit around a table and divide up the world for a hundred years to come. Now peace is not the product of a single conference but rather of continuous conversation.

2

There are some states of mind that make negotiation enormously difficult. And we have some of them. I believe many of our stereotypes about the Russians are mistaken. We regard them as undilutedly ideological and constantly plotting world revolution. I don't think they are. Whatever their long-term objective of a world safe for communism, in all current events there is a highly pragmatic side to their policies. They want good relations with Mr. Nehru; so they do not use the steel mill they are building in India as a base for propaganda. They do not embarrass France in Algeria. And they may even find Chinese aggressions in Asia embarrassing. They propose to sell their gem diamonds on the world market through those "imperialist capitalist exploiters," the international diamond cartel. When Western producers complain, they stop exporting aluminum at cut prices. One could multiply the instances. They add up to a careful Russian assessment of Russia's interests—of which ideology is only one.

Nor are they demons. With Stalin no doubt we were dealing with a madman whose manias took us to the fringes of hell. But with Mr. Khrushchev we are dealing with a realistic politician and polemicist. But I doubt if apocalyptic visions so darken his sight that we cannot conduct the dialogue of reason with him.

Nor, above all, are the Russians supermen. Sometimes when I read American accounts of Russian intentions and policies, I feel that I am studying a system of power so ruthlessly efficient and effective that our poor faltering democracies, our ponderous system of persuasion and consensus, had better give up in advance. Then I remember the Kremlin's unholy miscalculations of 1939, the near-collapse of 1941, the postwar seizure of Eastern Europe which turned the world's admiration into cold hostility, Tito's daring rebellion, the infinite difficulty of reversing a brutal dictatorship after Stalin, the uprisings of 1953 in East Germany, the Hungarian horror of 1956, the new uncertainties with China. This system—like ours—stumbles and feels its way. We must not hypnotize ourselves with the myth of its infallibility.

It seems to me both sad and ironic that the Communists have so largely succeeded in preempting and exploiting the cry for peace—which is surely the loudest and dearest sound in this war-weary, frightened world. They have been able to do so, not only because of their shameless use of propaganda and falsehood, but also because we underestimated mankind's yearning for peace. We have emphasized military containment, and for years it appeared that we didn't want to negotiate with the Russians, either to test their intentions or to call their bluff.

Meanwhile they stopped nuclear testing unilaterally; they reduced their army unilaterally; they proposed summit talks about reducing tensions and the dangers of war; they proposed total disarmament. Whatever the motive, cynical or sincere, they have constantly taken the initiative. They have answered the cry for peace, while we have quibbled and hesitated and then finally given in. Too often our approach has been "yes but" instead of "why not?" Too often our uncertainty and quibbling has left the impression that the United States is looking for reasons not to reach an agreement.

3

Security is not the only vital field in which our policies are confused and clouded by false or inadequate preconceptions. If we turn from disarmament as a preliminary to achieving the rule of law—our first international concern—to the other great issue of the world's general welfare, I think we find the same uncertainty of goals betraying itself in hesitations and inadequacies of performance. Since the Korean War the chief aim of our programs was, frankly, to stop the Communists. Recently, however, a new and more hopeful goal has appeared. Many of the West's leaders —President Dwight Eisenhower, Prime Minister Harold Macmillan, General Charles de Gaulle—have taken notice of the great and growing gap between the rich nations (largely in the Atlantic arena) and the poor who make up at least a billion souls in the lands outside the Communist bloc which are underdeveloped, unmodernized, and almost wholly lacking in the capital they need for growth. Many of us have long preached that economic development is as important to our security as military defense, and now our leaders have stated that bridging the gap must be a full Western responsibility.

This new emphasis on the positive task of building up the economies of the emergent peoples brings us within measurable distance of a genuine concept of solidarity and welfare. It is in every sense a welcome step forward. What troubles me is the evidence that little serious thought is being given by governments to the concrete strategies needed to turn the new aspiration into concrete policy.

To give two concrete examples—we have in the Indian development plans admirable instruments for transforming 40 per cent of the peoples living in the poorer lands into active productive citizens of a modern state. As in all developing economies, India cannot cover the foreign exchange element in its plans out of trade earning alone. And I could say many of the same things about Latin America, where we have no more loyal friends of freedom, and where the needs for foreign development capital are equally large.

But the Western nations have made no decision to see these great ventures through to success by a massive and sustained joint effort. Can our talk of our obligations to end the gap between the world's rich and the world's poor be treated seriously when our approach to any specific commitment still rests on a day-to-day basis, with no guarantee that we are ready to look beyond tomorrow's need—or tomorrow's crisis?

To my mind, the situation in Africa is quite as critical as in Asia. The ending of the old colonial links can mean the end of a large flow of public capital just as private enterprise hesitates to undertake new commitments in the face of political uncertainty. Have we a strategy for this situation? Is the end of Western control and the beginning of independence to coincide with massive impoverishments in Africa? If so, what better recipe could there be for Communist infiltration, what greater mockery of the West's claim to a constructive and modernizing role?

The universal complaint in South America and all these raw material exporting countries is the instability of prices for their metals, coffee, cotton, wool, and the other products that often constitute their major source of foreign exchange. Is it beyond the genius of free government and capitalist economy to stabilize some of these prices and give these countries some predictable continuity of income on which they can plan and build?

I could talk of other uncertainties—for instance, government often expecting private business to take political risks which go far beyond the responsibilities it can legitimately undertake; private enterprise in its turn showing an almost ideological distaste for government investment and "socialism" even where there is no capital to support capitalism in these underdeveloped countries.

So, if the balance of the world turned on the recovery of Europe and the success of the Marshall Plan twelve years ago, now it turns on North-South relations, to borrow General de Gaulle's phrase. But our separate economic strength is not great enough for the task of the industrial North in the developing South. We shall have to coordinate and cooperate and confederate—or whatever it is—to ensure that we have common economic policies on both sides of the Atlantic. We shall have to contrive adequate machinery to answer the many questions of how much investment is needed, where and in what priority it should be invested, how the burdens and benefits should be shared, and all the problems of planning and programming.

Such machinery is at hand at last. The Organization for Economic Cooperation and Development (OECD), which includes Western Europe, Canada, and the United States will, we hope, come into existence in 1961. And with it we can concert the mighty economic power of the West for the decisive challenge of the 1960's. Will we?

But perhaps the chief difficulty is also the most serious—the lack of public understanding of our assistance programs, the failure to give the American people any really constructive idea of what is being done in their name.

"Operation Rat Hole," "Wasting the taxpayers' money," "Paying foreigners to compete with us," "Giving away our jobs"—the chorus of articulate disapproval is constant.

Even though many citizens sincerely and consistently support the program, I wonder if half enough people really know the profound reasons for their continuance?

I believe the reasons can be made more than convincing. They can be made exciting. They can accord with our American tradition of an expanding frontier, of work to be done and hurdles to be leaped, of new markets to be opened in a challenging, exhilarating world. To complete the revolution of modernization which began in the West, to spread education to all peoples, to offer hope and health and good food and shelter and elbow room to all the members of our great human family—these are not negligible goals. They complete the vision of a Jefferson or a Lincoln—of burdens lifted from every shoulder and a life of opportunity for all mankind.

In this perspective, we can see the vast joint effort of bringing capital and trained manpower and technical skill to work in the emergent economies, not only as a world-wide extension of our principle of the general welfare, but as a new and exciting extension of our American dream, a new frontier, a new hope, a new achievement, a new pride.

4

Nor would I wish for a greater vision and a higher aim simply for ourselves. Am I wrong in supposing that in the world at large there is some latent desire to see expressed and practiced the policies which unite us, which express not our differences but our profound human needs, which give us something of our human solidarity, which leave our tribal feuding behind and remind us of the grandeurs and miseries of our shared destiny?

Here we are caught up in our horrible war games, in this gang warfare of a delinquent universe. But in our hearts—and perhaps in Communist hearts as well—there are times when we feel to the core war's idiocy and futility. We cannot give up our armaments separately. We are like two men in a dark room, each armed and feeling for the other. Neither dares put his weapon down for fear the other may not.

But as we grope in the dark, could we not reach for some other light to flood our narrow chamber, some fresh illumination of our aims and intentions which might enable us at last with confidence to put the ugly weapon aside? Light could come, I believe, from working together on projects really relevant to our profoundest human needs. We know what they are. They are not concerned with frontiers or nuclear weapons or matters of prestige. They deal with the fundamentals of our living— with the surge of population, with the expansion of food, the mobilization of resources, the direction of science to creative ends, the opening of the doors of knowledge, the banishment from outer space of the petty rivalries of earthbound man, the expansion of beauty in our lives—through competing in excellence, not in tons of metal or kilowatt-hours.

Such aims, more in keeping with the full dimensions of the human spirit, need not remain remote and disembodied. Why not propose to the Russians an international commission to tackle the problem of the world's greatest deserts? We are on the verge of achieving the desalinization of water on an economic scale. Why not work out the implications of this scientific breakthrough in some great arid area and do it jointly, creating as we go a new patrimony for the human race?

Why not make new preparations for a world-wide medical year; and after it, set up permanent commissions in vital fields of research to formalize the fact that in this of all fields all knowledge should be available to all men?

There are other areas. I hope the powers will quickly return to the conference table to work out an agreed law of the seas. Perhaps they could add to it a commission to establish rights and procedures to be followed when nations begin to probe under the oceans for new raw material supplies.

I trust, in short, that every opportunity we in the West can see to dramatize the common interests of humanity will be seized on and developed so that, whatever the obstructions put up by the Communists, the sense will spread through the world that the Western peoples are profoundly and permanently committed to the survival and dignity of man.

For in the last analysis, what else is of value, for ourselves and our children? These are visionary days in every field. We have unlocked the atom. We are laying bare the secrets of man's heredity. New infinite vistas have opened in space, new infinite abysms are opening backward in time. We have seen a rocket hit the moon. We know its dark face. Our astronauts wait to venture on a journey more mysterious than the quest of the Golden Fleece. We are adding a city a day to the world's population. How can we be content in such an age to keep our political thinking within the narrow bonds of class or race or nation? How can we permit outdated ideology to obscure our identity as citizens of a common world?

Our Western peoples must speak once again for man and for the human city. In doing so, they can save themselves—and their present adversaries. They may do more; they can begin to realize the full promise of this abundant but distracted world.

8

"THE WINDS OF CHANGE"

Lester B. Pearson

Tensions do not divide themselves neatly into compartments. So whatever we discussed, Legal Basis of International Order, Economic Development, Communications, shadowing all, and influencing all discussions, was the overriding political tension from which the others arise or by which they are influenced; this in its turn is caused by the fear and suspicion which exist between the two great power and ideological groupings in the world.

At the Chicago conference—in spite of, and not because of, the three-day concentration of unparalleled brain power on our objective—we did not come up with pat and clean-cut solutions to our problems, or for our tensions. There are none such to be found—even in an intellectual blitz of such energy and character.

I believe, however, that we left there clearer in our own minds about the nature and complexity of the tensions in the areas which we more specifically examined; and, more important, about the necessity, the urgency of doing something about them before they explode in our faces which we are so often preoccupied in saving. This urgency has a deeper meaning for us now—as a result of our exchanges there.

We realize—more than we did—that not the tensions, but the

circumstances, the situations, and the policies that produce them, are the real problem.

Tensions—when they are not convulsions—can be, and often are, a stimulus to progress. The alternative to them is not necessarily stability. It may be stagnation.

It is the control and direction of tensions into the right channels, as we have found out, that is the problem. Moreover it is one for which, at least in democratic societies, the individual and the community have as much, or more, responsibility than governments. Domestically and often internationally, we get the kind of tensions which we deserve and, at times, demand. This became quite clear in the consideration of the relationship between communications and tensions. Modern media of communications used for wrong purposes can increase and intensify such tensions in the individual, where it all starts; between individuals and groups within a nation; and, finally, between nations, often tense from their efforts and determination to protect their national interests, their national sovereignties, their prides, and sometimes their prejudices.

Another thing that emerged from our discussions—as it was bound to—was the smallness and the indivisibility of our world; and the oneness, whether we like it or not—and I confess that on occasions I don't myself get any particular joy out of it—the oneness of its inhabitants. I believe that there is far greater recognition of that fact today—how could there not be?—than ever before in history; recognition, that is, of a oneness that encompasses the whole planet; not the Greek world, the Roman world or the Holy Roman Empire. One world today means everybody.

We are now all kept *by*, and are keepers *of*, our brothers. That doesn't necessarily make for decrease of tensions but it may force us to do something about them.

There's the rub. What to *do* about them? In this case, as in many others, recognition is far ahead of result. An awareness of the necessity of building the political, economic, and legal institutions that this oneness requires has not been followed, in any adequate way, by action.

So what do we do now? How can we follow through? Circulate our reports? That may be useful; especially if we can get them into the hands of those who make and advise on government policy. There are ideas in them that are penetrating and practical and which should be examined by governments as a basis for national policies and international cooperation.

But that is not enough.

We can do more.

The "winds of change" are blowing in the world today—in more ways than we realize, and in more directions. They are blowing away old ideas, old concepts, as well as some old institutions. They are blowing creatively, as well as destructively.

They are blowing away the acceptance of nuclear war—and therefore any war—as something that is tolerable as a method of settling anything. They are also blowing away the assumption that old-fashioned methods of intergovernmental negotiation through diplomats and political representatives, whether at the summit, on the slopes, or on the level, are the only methods open to us. We are beginning to realize that they must be supplemented and spurred by new techniques of contact which take more realistically into account the changes in our societies and in our world.

I am thinking of meetings on the scientific and technical levels; nongovernmental. It is on these levels that international cooperation often most accurately reflects the new world we live in; the world where science has made inescapable the community of all men. Often those who operate within the old institutions and frameworks for international political and diplomatic contact are only partly aware of this new world; or, if they are aware of it, they are inhibited by the traditions and practices and conventions of the past. Official diplomatic conferences today can at times be closer to the Barons of Runnymede than to the Congress of Geophysicists.

More and more, nongovernmental meetings of scientists, technicians, experts, are underlining and helping to correct this anomaly. They have been perhaps the most successful mechanism for bridging the gulf between the two agglomerations of world power now interlocked in conflict and deadlocked because of it.

Peace must be more than the absence of destruction. It must be creative, not merely preventive. It must be used for progress; to bring about greater human welfare; to ensure the dignity and the equal rights of all members of the human family. Otherwise peace will not ensure the absence of the wrong kind of tensions.

We look beyond the new tensions that have come from recent incidents to the beginning of something better. We have had our shock treatment; let's begin the cure.

We must end the Cold War before some accident, or incident, makes it a war that could end us.

This is no holiday from history but a time for great achievement. It is also a challenge to our resolve—and our right—to survive.

Will leadership be equal to this challenge? Will the people be worthy of that leadership by refusing to accept less? Are we to leave the crusades to students marching and dying in the streets for national rights and freedoms? Is there no zeal and passion left for the great cause of peace among men?

9

SOME ACTIONS FOR PEACE *

A. To Strengthen the Law

Ernest A. Gross

The United States and the American people seek a world of peace and order. The institutions and processes of law can help achieve such a world, and reduce the tensions which trouble us. To strengthen the law must be regarded as a fundamental objective to ensure that nations can live in peace in an orderly community.

It is in the interest of all nations to avoid war and the use of force, and to exert every influence against the use of force by any nation anywhere.

There should be an intensified search for agreement on arms control and inspection. Both East and West must earnestly consider that there may be more security for them in less-than-perfect controls on armaments than in the fearful uncertainties of unbridled competition in the armaments of the future. For its part, the United States must recognize that perfect inspection is not possible, and that there is no real security today in the absence of arms control. The Government of the United States must in-

* Conclusions of The Conference on World Tensions held at the University of Chicago, May 11–13, 1960, as reported by the three Section Chairmen.

crease manyfold its efforts to explore the possibilities of inspection and control, multiplying the resources and energies which it is now devoting to this problem.

The authority and the potentialities of the United Nations for peaceful settlement must be enhanced. There is great promise, in particular, in the continued development of the mediation and good offices functions of the Secretary-General. Increased use of United Nations field representatives, of UN "presence" where appropriate, and administrative arrangements for a standby UN peace force, would contribute to this end.

There is need also for the development of new international law.

Coincidence of interest exists between the United States and the Soviet Union, as well as among all nations, to bar outer space to weapons of destruction, and to cooperate in the exploration and use of space for beneficial peaceful purposes. In other areas, too, there is need to anticipate the new law that will be called for by new technology. The United Nations affords both a context and an agency for developing such law.

There is need for new law in other situations where there is inadequate law, particularly where, in the past, nations sought recourse to force for lack of legal remedy. Adequate legal remedies should be developed for failure to meet financial or other contractual or treaty obligations to other nations, for mistreatment of their nationals, for endangering their important economic interests, and for interfering with communications. Flight over the territory of other nations creates tension, as do claims to use international waterways which are under national control. Racial discrimination and other denials of human rights evoke the legitimate concern of all nations. There is need for better law on such matters.

The reach of international law can be extended by "legislation," and by a natural, "common law" growth of practice and custom. Some codification may be desirable. The law should be collected, systematized, and made generally available by the UN and other agencies.

The new nations must be welcomed and assisted to take their place in an international community subject to international law.

The emergence of the new nations and their healthy and orderly development is inseparably related to our own welfare. We must assist them in finding a responsible place in a world community subject to laws and processes governing all nations. We must work with them to develop the concepts and scope of international law, to assure its applicability, in an atomic and space age, to new nations with differing racial, religious, and cultural origins and different economic situations and prospects.

The new nations will need sympathetic assistance to help them apply to their own situation the international law and practice of older nations, and to train their lawyers, administrators, and diplomats. There is urgent need also to train young leaders of these nations in the traditions of representative government, of individual freedoms and rights under law, modified as need be to meet local conditions and mores.

These ends can be furthered through special cultural technical assistance, so far as possible through the United Nations. Private institutions, including leading American law schools and Bar Associations, should also contribute by sending consultants and teachers and providing libraries and other educational materials.

The United States should take the lead in extending the rule of law among like-minded nations.

Under pressure of the tensions of the East-West conflict, the United States has not maintained its leadership toward the rule of law. The barely-escaped Bricker Amendment; the genocide convention buried in the Senate; the indifferent participation in the activities of the International Law Commission and of the Legal Committee of the General Assembly; the abandonment

and avoidance of efforts to establish common international standards by multilateral agreement—these are but examples.

This trend must be reversed. Groups of states—for example, the
United States, the United Kingdom and Canada, and other nations
willing to join with them—should establish a well developed rule of
law as an example to all nations. This would include increased
use of the International Court of Justice. Recourse to the Court
should not be regarded as a hostile act. Greater use of the Court
will contribute to its growth and to the expansion of international
legal doctrine.

In connection with the use of the Court, the United States
has set a deplorable example. The Connally Amendment should
be repealed. It is improper in principle. Because of the applicable
rule of reciprocity, it has also hurt the United States by giving
the same power to deny the jurisdiction of the Court to any State
which the United States might wish to sue. Nor is the reservation
of value to the United States. Withdrawing it would not increase
substantially the extent to which the United States is subject
to the International Court of Justice. Its repeal would remove
a continuous reminder of United States reluctance to submit
to international adjudication.

In this as in other areas, leadership by the United States requires the support of enlightened public opinion. To this end, consideration should be given to the formal organization of a body
of private citizens, staffed so as to be available for consultation and
advice to the government in the field of international law.

In a world of tensions, the perfect "rule of law" is a distant objective. Treaties with ideal provisions will not be signed; courts will
not be endowed with extensive jurisdiction over all nations and
issues, nor will they be fully used or faithfully obeyed. Nevertheless, through the use of concepts, institutions, and methods of law,
war can be avoided, specific sources of tension can be eliminated,
and the breadth and depth of order among nations can be increased. In the nuclear space age, this is essential to survival.

B. To Complete the Revolution of Modernization

Paul G. Hoffman

Some way must be found to convince the high-income countries of the world that economic development of the low-income countries has not yet been accorded the priority it demands.

It is far more important to most of the world's people than the issues that consume weeks of high-level discussion at meetings of foreign ministers and chiefs of state. Talk about these issues we must, but it is quite as imperative that the richer countries act more vigorously in assisting economic growth in Asia, Africa, and Latin America, with serious intent and soon.

To the poorer countries, in which two-thirds of the world's people live, the most pressing concern is to improve living standards and thus their sense of dignity and independence—a task made more difficult in crucial areas by the overwhelming press of population.

To the richer countries, the active revolt of these peoples against the continued acceptance of poverty, illiteracy, and chronic ill health presents moral and political issues of the first magnitude. For they must:

1. Accept the fact of Soviet economic growth and consequent Soviet participation in world economic development.

2. Improve the complex of institutions that serve as a bridge between richer and poorer countries in the stimulation of economic development.

3. Provide the added resources—both things and people—to help build within the poorer countries the institutions and conditions required for economic growth.

Soviet bloc aid to underdeveloped countries takes the form of increased trade and credits. It can represent a net addition to the resources available to build up the stock of capital in the poor countries; therefore these credits are not necessarily to be deplored, either from the standpoint of the recipient countries or that of the Free World.

Soviet bloc countries might even be urged to increase their aid, particularly that part channeled multilaterally. Aid so channeled would be completely removed from the Cold War context.

There is room in the broad and complex task of economic development for many channels of help from the high-income countries to the low-income countries.

Bilateral programs of technical and economic assistance have been developed by several countries, and in some cases are the most effective way to meet evident needs. Many voluntary organizations such as foundations, unions, churches, associations, and a host of private investors also make useful and unique contributions. Then there are the regional organizations, such as the Colombo Plan and the Inter-American Development Bank, and finally, the multinational organizations, such as the United Nations and the specialized agencies.

While all have their place, it is clear that greatly expanded use should be made of the services of the multinational agencies. In sensitive areas, aid from multinational agencies is more acceptable politically. Recipient nations accept from a multinational agency conditions which they would regard as onerous coming from a single nation. Such assistance is, moreover, a completely cooperative endeavor, with a voice given to countries whatever their size or wealth and all countries contributing to the cost.

The very variety of agencies requires much more coordination of private, national, and international efforts to assist each emergent country. This can best be accomplished in each country by the development of an over-all country program to which all types of assistance must be related. The chief United Nations economic representative in each country is uniquely placed to work with the recipient country in developing such a program.

Economic development involves social, political, economic and psychological factors about which there is much yet to learn. There is need for a substantial expansion in basic research in all these disciplines.

However, we do know that there is:

1. Insufficient knowledge of the natural resources of poor countries.

2. Insufficient trained manpower.

3. Lack of capital.

Most of these needs will ultimately be met by the poor countries' own efforts. It is clear, however, that these countries are not now receiving as much external aid as they could use effectively. It is also clear that the rich countries are not now providing as much assistance as they can afford to do and should do.

If a reasonable rate of economic growth is to be attained in the 1960's, poor countries will need, in addition to self-supplied resources, additional external aid of about $3 billion a year, of which $1 billion could well be from increased private investment and bankable loans.

The questions remain: what is the motive that can be expected to support, in the high-income countries, an adequate increase in assistance to their low-income neighbors in the world? Specifically, if more of an enlarged total amount is channeled through international agencies, will the electorates of the Western democracies find in their hearts and in their politics a persuasive supporting motivation?

It is the nature of societies built on variety and tolerance to take "next steps" from a mixture of motives. Foreign aid programs have already benefited from the combined strength of two rationales—national security and humanitarian good will—which may seem on the surface to be opposed to each other.

Now, with a decade and a half of experience behind us, we can see more clearly two related but additional motivations for action by the richer countries: It is in the interest of them all that their poorer neighbors should be prosperous—so we should contribute to making that prosperity possible. And insofar as the richer countries have unused resources—which nearly all of them do—it is in their interest to use these resources "to complete the revolution of modernization which began in the West." Out of the massive yearnings of the hundreds of millions of people for a better life can come a better world, or if their yearnings are ignored, a world of mounting and explosive tensions.

C. To Ease the Passage of Persons and Ideas

Barry Bingham

Communication, as we have come to use the word, involves all contact between peoples—whether personal, or through the flow of information and ideas.

The inhibition of such contacts in itself constitutes a major threat to peace.

Saying this, however, does not imply a simple belief that reduction of the barriers to communication alone would reduce world tensions and eliminate the prospect of a final holocaust.

The problems of communication are the direct product of deep-seated political divisions among nations, and of ideological, religious, and cultural differences among peoples. The international tensions associated with these problems may in time be eased by technological progress and change, but so far the evidence indicates that the process has accentuated them. Rapidly improving means of communication have shrunk our world, and will continue to do so, but the mere drawing together of people cannot in itself reduce tensions. On the contrary, new proximity may make hitherto remote possibilities of conflict of interest seem, and perhaps be, imminent; the reduction of the ocean barriers by the airplane and the rocket has created new demands for national security—and these demands, more often than not, have been met by restrictions on the free passage of persons and ideas.

No one can rationally dismiss the problems of security that confront most nations today. But one can inquire whether the present restrictions on communications have not long since passed beyond the outer limits of prudence—whether, in fact, they have not come to be dictated more by purely political considerations than by the legitimate demand for protection against espionage, sabotage, or internal disruption.

The fact is that the recent breakthroughs—significant as they may be—have come as a result of sustained haggling between governments, without apparent regard for any principle higher than *quid pro quo*.

Acknowledging the hazards, recognizing the practical difficulties, unbemused by any false hope of quick and easy salvation, our general conclusions are these:

• It should be the urgent business of every government to work toward the reduction of restrictions on communication to the lowest practical level.

• It should be the urgent business of the peoples of all countries to urge this course upon their governments.

In the end, practical progress toward these goals will involve multilateral action by concerned nations, and by private persons and groups within the several nations.

What do these very general principles mean for the posture and practices of the United States, both official and private? At a minimum, they mean:

1. Any effort on the part of the United States or any nation to break through existing barriers to communications by unilateral action based solely on acceptance of its own concepts or practices, would prove futile, and any such effort would in itself contribute to world tensions.

2. In many important respects the communications systems of the United States, and of the Western world, do not practically mesh with those of other nations. These differences are not alone philosophical, and they are not confined to the nations which have adopted or accepted Communist ideology. The difficulties are also frequently encountered in relationships with nations newly come to statehood, and older nations which have never followed the practices of an open society.

3. These differences must be taken into account in any action aimed at reducing the barriers to international communications. Practical results can be obtained only by a meeting of concerned nationals, whether private citizens or representatives of government or a mixture of the two, on an equal footing. (But the United States should not seek accord with other countries, at the price of compromise or accommodation that commits it to anything less than the full freedom of press and of speech assured in the Constitution. While taking account of the difficulties of achieving that full freedom elsewhere, the struggle to gain it universally ought never to be relaxed. We cannot settle for a lower level of liberty in the world, either for ourselves or for others.)

4. As a manifest of its own faith in the ultimate benefits to be derived from improved communications, the United States should remove, or reduce to the lowest practical level, its own restrictions

upon the temporary entry and free movement of foreign nationals, and upon the movement of United States nationals abroad. The only acceptable limitations should be those based on clearly demonstrated requirements of national security.

5. The principles applied to maximum practical freedom of movement for persons should also apply to the flow of information.

6. Political and military limitations on communications, such as those occasioned by the lack of diplomatic relationship between the United States and Communist China, should be ameliorated in every practical way.

7. Under the best conditions obtainable in a divided world, the private systems of disseminating information upon which the United States properly places its reliance in internal affairs are not adequate for international communications. The private systems, therefore, must be supplemented by direct government action in the field of information. The evolution and acceptance of a continuing policy based upon the principle underlying the present program of the United States Information Agency are therefore essential.

8. Similarly, official barriers and economic differentials among the nations make it necessary that the United States government adopt as a continuing policy the principle underlying the present programs involving international exchange of persons.

9. While recognizing the soundness of the principle involved in these programs, we find that neither is presently buttressed by a stable and coherent operating policy. A division of popular opinion is reflected in Congress on the fundamental question of whether these programs should have been initiated in the first place, and should now be continued in any event. In addition, excessive concern with security considerations has proved a major handicap in the exchange of persons. These are the fundamental causes of the wavering policy lines and of the fluctuation in appropriations. Adequate support for these programs requires strong and

forthright leadership in the administration and the Congress, and maximum support by concerned private agencies and individuals.

10. Although the government must assume the major burden of financing the exchange of persons, it should continue to rely wherever possible upon established private organizations for the actual operation of the program. Although the government has not attempted to interfere at the higher policy levels concerning the arrangements made for visiting foreign nationals by these agencies, excessive bureaucratic restrictions upon the allocation and expenditure of funds have proved a major hindrance. Also these programs have suffered in some instances from lack of adequate planning at the initial point of contact between governments. A review of these programs, and correction of these deficiencies, should precede any expansion. An increase in the quantity of these exchanges may be desirable, but not at the expense of the quality of the program.

11. Means should be sought to make maximum use of the facilities of the United Nations in the dissemination of information and in the exchange of persons. To that end the supporting governments should immediately make available funds to provide for the speedy reproduction and transmittal of official transcripts of proceedings and related matter, as is normally done in the case of the deliberations of the governing bodies of individual nations.

Although these conclusions deal for the most part with official action, we should not underestimate the importance of private activity in the area of communications. Indeed, it might be argued that the ideal we seek is an international society so open that official action would no longer be required to encourage or facilitate contact between peoples and the flow of information and ideas.

Private foundations, and educational, cultural, religious, and professional organizations are now making major contributions toward international understanding. Because they can operate without the restraints of official formality, and because they can promote associations and exchanges based upon practical mutual interests, it is possible to hope that they are setting patterns for the future. Certainly the greatest value comes from international organizations formed through the impetus of concerned individuals rather than through the stimulation of governments.

A notable example is the newly formed international association of anthropologists which now reaches into every major nation except Communist China. Operating on a modest grant from a private foundation and served only by a volunteer staff, the organization has provided a clearinghouse for professional information through publication of a member-written periodical. Out of this have come working personal contacts among anthropologists whose personal convictions range across the whole of the political spectrum, but who are bound together by their mutual professional interest. Similar examples may be cited in the expanding areas of communication among scientists.

However, in the present state of affairs, action by government is essential—both in terms of necessary diplomatic support to open up the clogged channels of communication, and in terms of financial support for programs to ease the passage of persons and ideas, whenever such programs are beyond the scope of philanthropists and private agencies. Philosophically repugnant though this condition may be to some Americans, it is a fact of life that cannot be ignored.

AFTERWORD

Harlan Cleveland

The 1960 Conference on World Tensions met two months before the Congo crisis was heated to the boiling point by Soviet intervention; four months before the 1960 session of the United Nations General Assembly; six months before the 1960 election in the United States. These events, taken together with the fiasco at the summit in May, make 1960 something of a watershed.

Before 1960, some people still believed that the "search for peace" was mostly a matter of words, of negotiations and persuasion and speeches and technical discussions and legal debating points. After 1960, for Americans and their partners in the Western world, such a belief is a form of self-destruction. We have passed (hardly realizing it) from the era of *foreign relations* to the era of *foreign operations*.

For such an era we need a new agenda for peace, fit for the kind of international relations that consist in the mutual involvement of whole societies with each other's internal affairs. The starting point is a set of modern attitudes about foreign affairs, which are so painfully no longer the foreigners' affairs. Some of the specific actions are still lost in the murk of technical staff work; but the relevant attitudes are plain:

1. We cannot afford to be unimaginatively preoccupied with

our relations with the Russians and the Chinese, at the expense of our relations with the rest of the world. If we allow ourselves to become mesmerized by the Kremlin's antics, we find ourselves spending precious time talking about subjects of the Kremlin's choosing, rather than acting on subjects chosen by the free nations.

2. We need to build into our foreign policy a basic assumption of rapid political and social change in every foreign country—and in our own.

We are still tempted to refer to our international goals with words like "survival" and "stability"—static, stagnant words which imply that the best we can hope for is a slow deterioration of the world we like to live in. Seeing ourselves among the world's conservatives, we have tried to conserve old regimes and reactionary strong men that are destined to be swept away by man's scientific inventiveness and his aspirations for equality and freedom. It is, of course, a lost cause. Radical change is in the air. The question that faces Americans is whether we are going to sniff the new wind or suffocate in our own air-conditioned corner of the world.

3. We need to build the kinds of strength, concentrated at the "point of sale" in each developing country, that can most directly be converted into governmental institutions staffed with people who know, or at least are trying to learn, how to govern. This means a new look at our U.S. military and economic aid programs, and better ways of pulling them together in each country to make them pay off in viable governments and growing participation by peoples in their own governments. The world's power structure will change in freedom's favor as we act to make freedom worth while in the areas we can reach with our extraordinary (if as yet ill managed) influence. The word about how successfully free institutions are doing will seep through Curtains, Iron and Bamboo, soon enough; "liberation" will come not by military rollback but by making the free world hum with expanding opportunity and growing hope—the revolutionary sounds of success.

4. We must cure ourselves of talking about international peace as if it were merely a goal or objective, rather than a long, difficult, intense, and never-ending task of building international and regional institutions for cooperative action. "Peace" as a goal has been so large a tent that under it, during the 1950's, a Khrushchev could snuggle comfortably up to an Eisenhower. A practical peace policy will think of "peace" not merely as law but as institutions —a collective security force in Korea, an OAS resolution on Castro, a policing force under United Nations command in the Congo, a common attack on poverty through technical aid, a World Bank for large-scale investment and a UN Special Fund for preinvestment financing, a technical conference with other nuclear powers about bomb-testing, a mass education movement among illiterate peoples, a European Common Market or a Jordan Valley Authority or a regional development bank. While our 1960 national political conventions were debating platform planks, as many as eighty different public international councils, commissions, committees, or conferences were going on—and another eighty private international groups were meeting on every conceivable subject from irrigation to linguistics. These, together with the institutions of free government inside each country, are the building blocks of international community; a sense of community cannot be prefabricated at a summit conference.

For Americans, whose forefathers brought forth upon a new continent a nation built more on action than on political theory, it should not be too hard to get used to an operational way of looking at foreign policy. On the record, we have in 1960 discussed our "national purposes" much more than the actions we might take to carry them out. Yet most of the writers in a 1960 "National Purpose" series in *Life* magazine and *The New York Times* seemed to be saying something like this: There is nothing wrong with our national purposes that acting on them with imagination and vigor will not cure.